CHARACTER
DESIGN
MADE EASY

CHARACTER DESIGN MADE EASY

A COMPLETE COURSE TO CREATING ICONIC AND MEMORABLE CHARACTERS

DAVID & CHARLES
—PUBLISHING—

www.davidandcharles.com

CONTENTS

INTRODUCTION

Some of the most fun I had as a kid was not just drawing pictures, but imagining stories, ideas, and characters. Throughout life, that fun has only grown, and no doubt you've picked up this book because the same feeling rings true for you, too. Whether you want to create a career out of drawing and visual storytelling, or just want to express yourself through the imagined worlds and characters you create, you've found safe harbor here.

The problem is that ideas are often the easiest part—how we execute those ideas, typically through drawing, requires building up a skill we may not have fully formed yet. Maybe we don't know how to tell a story people care about. Or, we're simply lacking the visual vocabulary to communicate who our characters are effectively. These three pillars of Character Design, namely DRAWING, STORY, and DESIGN, are built upon throughout this book—reinforcing and supporting each other so that you can become confident in your ability.

While there are many ways to create characters, including 3D modeling and the like, this book seeks to help your drawing skills first and foremost. I have found that drawing is a discipline that helps things outside of the two dimensional. While I prefer to use digital tools for efficient drawing and illustrating, specifically the app Procreate on an iPad Pro, the majority of this book uses simple pencil and paper. The final chapter, which gets into color and rendering, uses examples from Procreate, however,

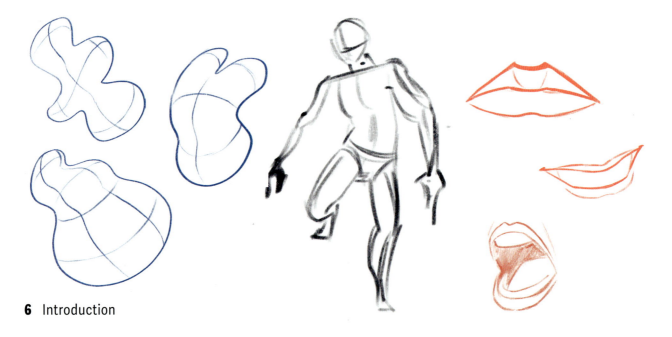

most digital art apps utilize a similar system of layers and layer styles, which will translate fairly seamlessly. I encourage you to draw along with the Warm-ups and Exercises included, so that you can build your skills to meet your dreams.

Character Design has not only been a tool that's let me work with major brands over the years, it's also helped me to make my own animated series and stories a reality. One of the characters from that series, Biko, will join you on your journey through this book. Character Design is a part of visual storytelling that is powerful—it transcends the medium it's a part of and creates a person in the mind of our viewer, one with a character and history like any real person. I hope this book makes that power a little more real to you. Enjoy!

This is Biko, he'd like to become a character designer too.
He works a day job as a medic, so it's probably a good idea for him to change into another outfit.

Let's take the journey to become a character designer together with Biko, starting with...

Chapter One:

DRAWING CHARACTERS

LINES AND SHAPES

All characters are made up of lines and shapes. This means that, as artists, we need to be able to draw lines and shapes well.

Character designs range from simplified and abstract, to complex and realistic.

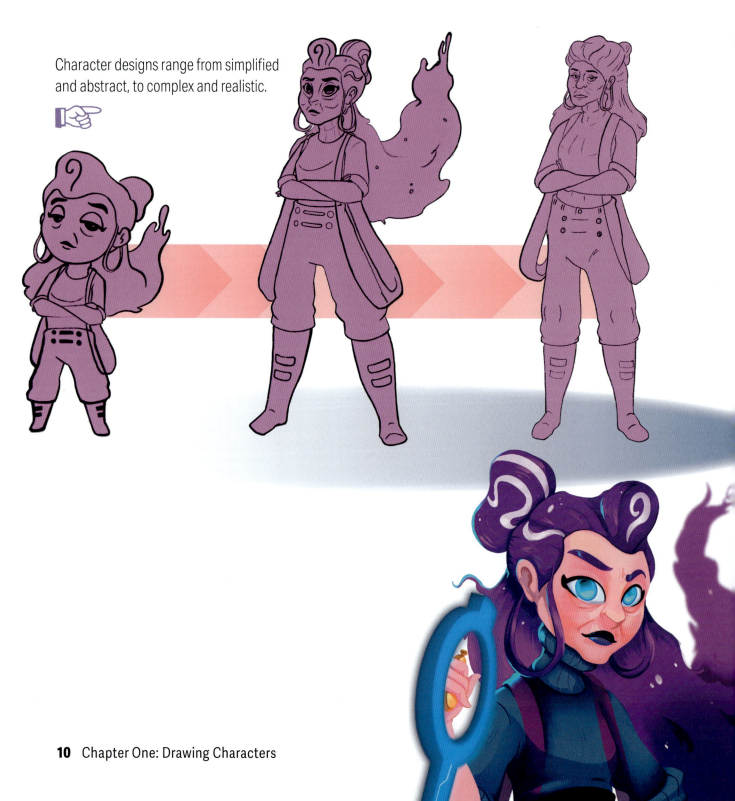

Usually, an artist who wants to draw characters in a stylized or simplistic way thinks they only need to learn how to draw things in that stylized way.

In reality, no matter how simple or complex, realistic or cartoony, anime or otherwise, all artists create better work when they learn the fundamentals of drawing.

The more you understand this:

The better you'll be at drawing this:

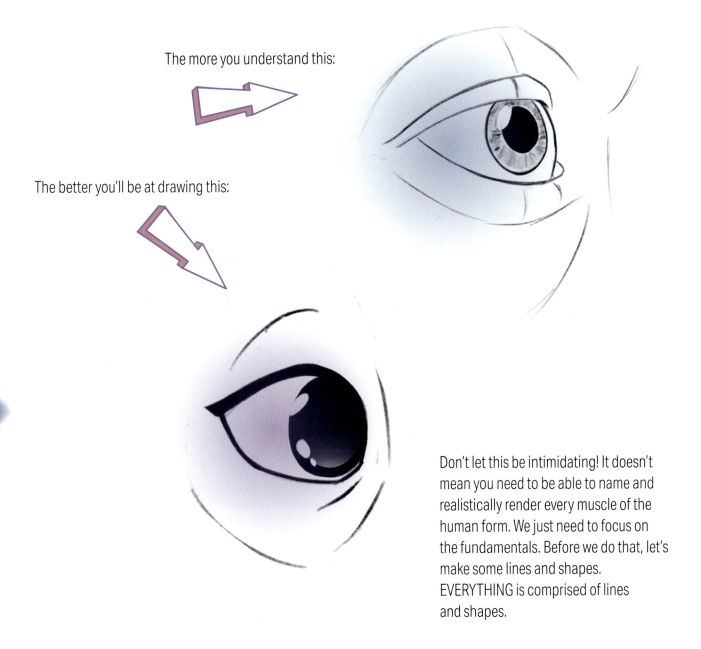

Don't let this be intimidating! It doesn't mean you need to be able to name and realistically render every muscle of the human form. We just need to focus on the fundamentals. Before we do that, let's make some lines and shapes. EVERYTHING is comprised of lines and shapes.

Draw with your whole arm, not just with your wrist

If you rest your wrist on a drawing surface, you will only be able to rotate in a small radius. But if you're drawing with your arm, you can get better control over your drawing muscles, and a larger range of movement.

When you begin to draw, remember you're using three things at once: your eyes, your brain, and your arm.

Let's first focus on the arm, and by extension, the hand.

But that feels weird! It's not what I'm used to!

You can still use your wrist for small detail lines, but most artists draw too small. Don't worry about getting used to it though, since that's our next step.

Warm-up: Lines

Sit with good posture and your drawing surface in front of you. One at a time, draw straight lines horizontally and vertically on the page. Try to keep them as straight as possible. Don't rush through it. If you mess up, that's okay. Simply try to take control of your drawing.

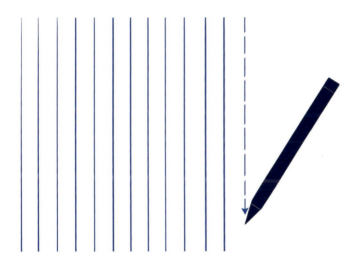

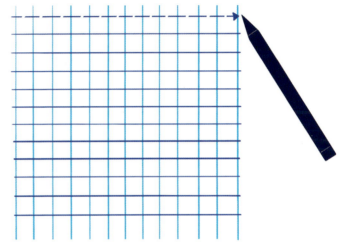

This is an exercise I do EVERY DAY that I sit down to draw. It helps calibrate my arm and mind to drawing. Feel free to make diagonal lines in either direction on this page as well. You might find that the lines that you pull toward your body are cleaner than the ones you push away from your body. This likely has to do with what our muscles are used to, and which ones are stronger.

Great start, Biko! You'll get better every time you do this exercise.

Warm-up: Shapes

On the same drawing surface, I usually like to add circles. These are circles that begin and end once, not circled around and around. Do your best to slowly make the best circle you can. Make them in all sizes, large and small. Try to make them clockwise AND counter-clockwise. Take note of which ones feel easier to you, and which ones are engaging the muscles in your hand and arm.

Don't worry about the practice you do in these warm-ups looking pristine or social media-ready. The point of practice is not to make a final product, it's to improve the act of doing something, and hopefully even understand it better!

If you combine circles and straight lines, you'll get the building blocks of all drawings. In fact, you can even use these tools to make flat, graphic characters, much like a certain Japanese cat.

However, these examples come across rather sterile and lifeless. There's two main things that are apparent: first, they're flat, and second, the shapes don't have any variety, tapering, or movement. Let's address that first problem on the next page.

FORMS

To really get the most out of our drawings, we need to understand the third dimension. This means creating depth on what is otherwise a flat piece of paper. But how? Let's start by turning our shapes into 3D forms.

This square is laying flat on the page in front of you. It probably even has a boring personality.

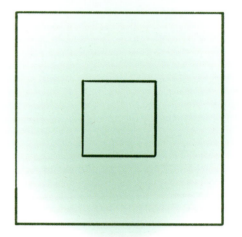

But what if we wanted this square to be an entrance to a tunnel that goes through this book? We would probably add a second square that is smaller inside it, because the exit to the tunnel is further away from us.

We have the entrance and exit, but in order to draw the tunnel itself, we need to connect the corners of these squares with straight lines.

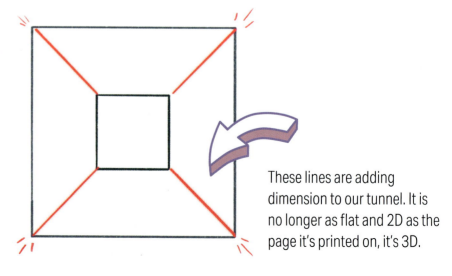

These lines are adding dimension to our tunnel. It is no longer as flat and 2D as the page it's printed on, it's 3D.

The lines we added can be called PERSPECTIVE LINES, and in this case, the tunnel we've made is called one point perspective. Why? Notice that all of these lines, if you kept drawing them, would eventually converge together in one point. That also means any lines of perspective we want to draw would START at this point.

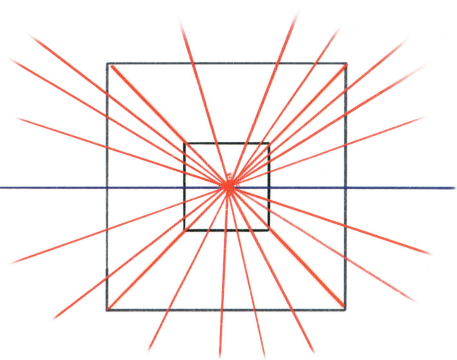

It feels like you're trying to trick me into like, doing math or something. I just wanted to draw characters.

Don't be intimidated by perspective, Biko! We don't need to make it complicated. Perspective is simply making a 3D space to put our drawings in, and to give our drawings context. It's depth and dimension.

For example: if we made a line halfway through our tunnel horizontally on the floor, we would know roughly how far something is away from us. If a mouse was standing at the entrance, it would appear to be half the size down the tunnel.

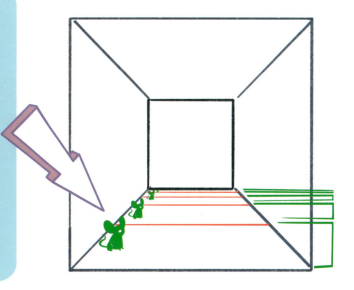

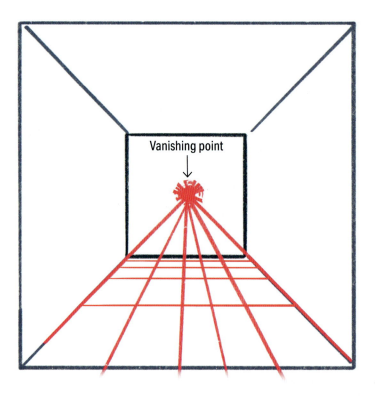

Things get smaller as they reach the "point" in our one point perspective—that's why it's called a vanishing point. If you went outside in a flat desert, and watched your friend walk into the horizon, eventually they would get so small they'd disappear.

What does this have to do with characters?

Our tunnel is just one use of what we call a constructed shape. Construction takes flat shapes and makes them 3D. This tunnel is nothing special, it's simply a box! We can rotate this box any way we like. But before we do that...

Rotating a Square

A square is flat, but we can rotate it from the top, as if we were flipping a coin.

When you rotate a square, our perspective dictates what it will look like at other angles.

These basic shapes may seem simple or boring at first, but the better we are at understanding and representing them, the better artists we'll be.

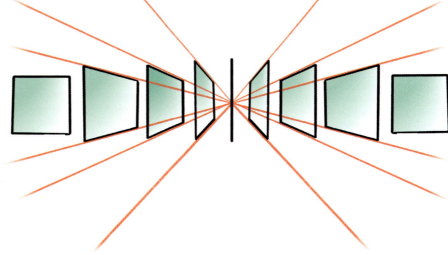

If the perspective is SHALLOW, the end of the square that's further from us will be close in size to the end that's near us.

If the perspective is EXTREME, the end of the square will be much smaller. It ends up looking more like you're drawing a long rectangle.

Take note of how far away the point of our perspective is from each square.

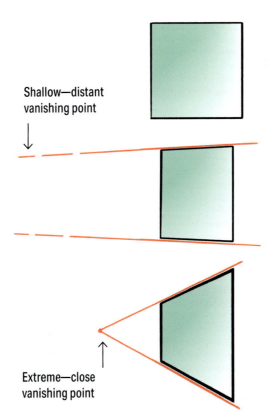

Shallow—distant vanishing point

Extreme—close vanishing point

Exercise 1

Practice rotating this square in space. You can do so side to side, like on the previous page, or from top to bottom. Try to make the size of the square consistent.

BONUS: if you have access to a frame-by-frame animation application, you can do this exercise there, and use it to see how smooth your results look in motion!

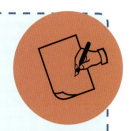

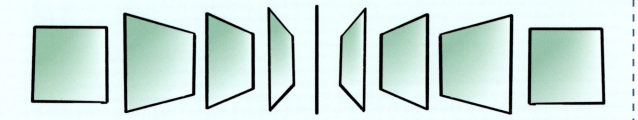

"I KNEW there'd be math!"

Constructing Shapes

Construction is simply taking a shape like the one you've just made, and adding another shape from another dimension.

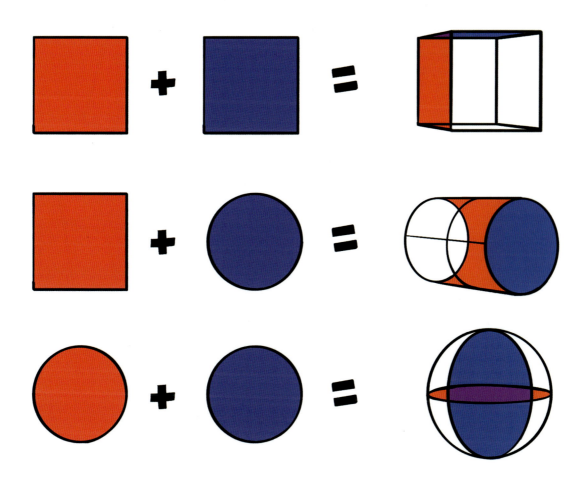

There are other shapes you can make, but these are the basic building blocks that are used to make all characters! The extra lines that exist inside the shape are called CONTOUR LINES. They're there to inform us of the third dimension. The best part is, we can use these to start with, then cut into and add onto our constructed shapes from there.

The better we are able to rotate these shapes in 3D space, the better we understand everything we draw.

Exercise 2

Rotate a cube the same way you previously rotated a square. All four sides are changing as it rotates. Feel free to "overdraw" the straight lines that are used to create the cube, as though they're perspective lines that all converge in one place. It will also be helpful for our upcoming sections to find the center lines in each direction of each plane of the cube.

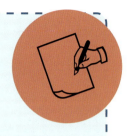

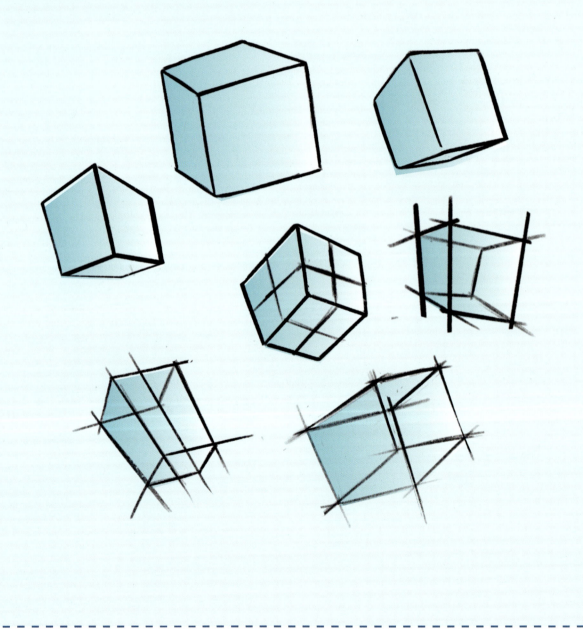

Exercise 3

Observe your surroundings and draw BOUNDING BOXES of what you see. Then fill them with the objects inside. Try to make sure the orientation and dimension of the objects makes sense in perspective.

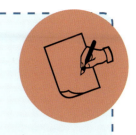

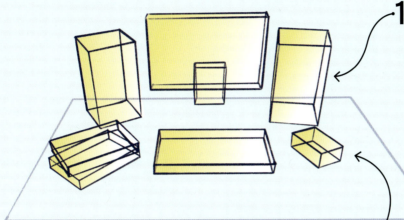

1 If you LOOK at your surroundings, you will likely see things that are either rectangular prisms or cubes exactly, are square in shape, or could at least be broken up into square shapes.

For example, a pile of books, a computer and keyboard, and a pair of speakers on a desk are just our bounding boxes in different shapes.

2 But the computer mouse, despite being round, can also fit into a box. That's because we know the way it's pointed. The bottom plane, or rectangle, of its box, is flat on the desk. The rest of its box can follow suit.

3 Now when we go to add the curves of the computer mouse, we can do that inside the box. This outer box we've made to contain something that isn't otherwise strictly a cube is called a bounding box. This quickly shows us the dimensions and orientation of any given object. This will be very useful for us as we draw many things, especially human anatomy.

I hate to be a bother, but a little help would be lovely!

Orienting a Sphere

When you draw spheres, remember that the contour lines are trying to show the right dimension. If you're drawing two contour lines, they should match each other. Too thin, or too tall, and you're breaking the 3D.

When you rotate a sphere, the outline, or silhouette, doesn't change. But our contour lines do.

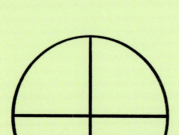 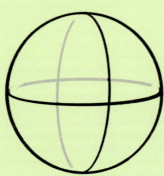 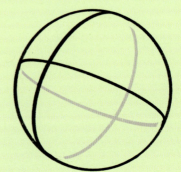

This is important, because these lines can help us to know where something on the surface of the sphere should be placed, like a nose!

Hey, look! That nose is a box too, and it's changing as we rotate it.

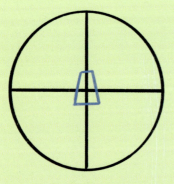 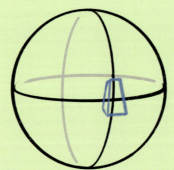 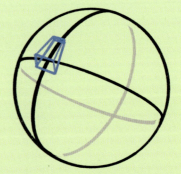

Exercise 4

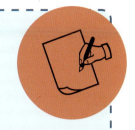

Draw spheres that are all "pointing" in different directions, like the angles of our cubes. Make sure to keep the contour lines consistent!

Once you're comfortable with this, you can either erase or not draw any part of the contour line that's disappearing behind our object. In other words, you can turn off the X-ray!

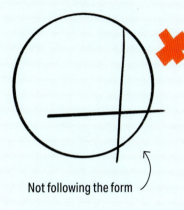

Not following the form

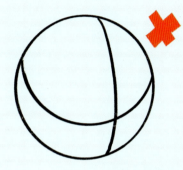

Following the wrong form

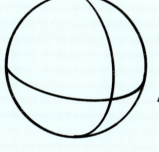

Wrapping believably around the existing form!

But... I don't have any bones?

This isn't about you, Biko.

Warm-up: Get Silly

We're about to take our constructed shapes to the next level, but before we keep trying to be precise and correct with what we draw, remember to stay loose as well. Here's another warm-up I like to do, drawing abstract, curving shapes, like this:

Sometimes I like to treat these shapes a little like stones in a wall, where they join up next to each other with enough room for mortar between them. Oftentimes, I will try and make faces out of these shapes! These are far sillier than anything that I'm intentionally trying to make into a legitimate character design. That's okay! They're just for fun.

They don't have to make much sense. The idea here is to keep some whimsy and fun in your drawings. That life and energy will come through in the characters you make, and is necessary to imbue them with a little bit of SOUL! Plus, I like to think of this as a stretch or loosening up exercise after being very careful and intentional with our straight lines and (attempts at) perfect circles. The idea of quickly drawing something that captures the motion of something, rather than the exact dimensions of it, is called GESTURE. We'll talk more about it later, but gesture is the opposite of construction, balancing it out and keeping it in check.

SUMMARY

While the things we've talked about in this chapter may seem very basic, they cover some of the most important fundamentals to our drawing ability, and affect our character design substantially.

Whenever you're returning to drawing after a break, or find your skills difficult to access, I highly recommend revisiting the steps over the last few pages, and attempting to deepen your understanding of each concept.

Remember, drawing well is about observing, understanding, and executing well, with your eyes, brain, and muscles.

Chapter Two:

DRAWING ANATOMY

BODY BASICS

It's possible you have no intention to draw human characters. You might think that makes this section easy to skip over. DON'T. You might want to skip this section because you don't plan on drawing people realistically. Again: DON'T.

While realism is valuable, studying anatomy in Character Design is all about understanding proportions, and representing parts of the body in believable, easily recognizable ways. These principles will carry over and strengthen EVERY kind of character design you do. So DON'T skip this chapter!

The Head and Skull

The better we understand and can represent the human body, the better all our characters will be. That's doubly important with the human head. Why?

First of all, we've all seen a LOT of human heads. It gets pretty easy to tell when a drawing of one doesn't look quite right.

Second, we all LOOK at human heads to understand one—we might read someone's lips, study their facial expressions, or lock eyes with them. It's one of the main ways we communicate! If you want your characters to visually communicate well, you should understand their primary instrument for communicating.

Human heads have so much variety of appearance, affected by muscle, fat, genetics, and positioning of certain features. However, there is one constant that doesn't vary: the skull. All skulls are very similar to one another, only changing proportionately as a baby ages into a child, and then into an adult. That means we can use the same basic construction for them, in order to study and understand them.

Artists have come up with many different methods for drawing the head, so you can achieve the right outcome via many paths.

TOP VIEW

THREE-QUARTER VIEW

First things first, the skull is not a perfect sphere! It's oblong, like an oval. If you feel your own head, you might notice that it's flat on the sides. That means we can start either with a sphere that we flatten the sides of, or start with a cylinder that we add roundness to on the front, top, and back.

SIDE VIEW

 Next, we want to start building in the jaw—this can be done with a simple box on the front of the face. But we aren't done yet!

 Our face isn't flat. Our eyes are recessed into our head and are protected by the ocular bones. We can cut a sort of wedgelike shape out of the area where our eyes are, to show an approximation of this recess.

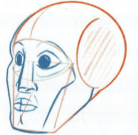
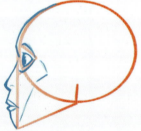

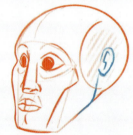
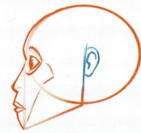

 Our mouth, along with our nose, juts forward slightly. The side of our face isn't usually round, either, but has a certain trapezoidal angle, shown here.

 Ears start just behind the top of the jaw, so we can follow the line of the jaw up and use it as the front of our ear.

Facial Features

Once you've drawn the skull and face, add facial features—the eyes, nose, and mouth—to build the identity of your character through expression.

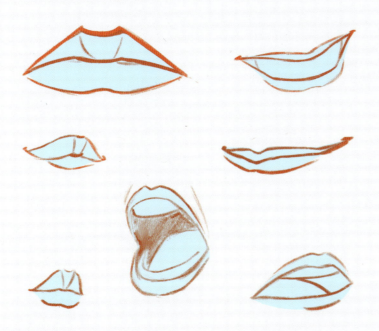

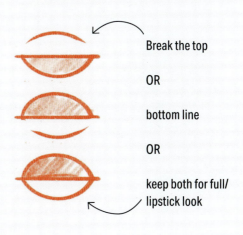

Break the top

OR

bottom line

OR

keep both for full/lipstick look

☞ The mouth and lips are more than just squiggly lines, we can study lips to find that they are constructed shapes themselves!

Exercise

This is a big one, but it's essential. Draw a total of 50 heads using the method opposite. Draw from lots of different angles. Observe real people, or pictures of them, and find the patterns and repeating shapes in the head and face. The idea is to download this visual library into your brain, so that you can easily repeat it.

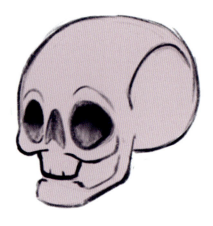
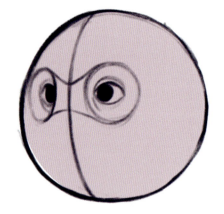

 The ocular bones around the eyes on the skull serve as a protection to the sensitive eyeballs—that means the eyes are recessed into the head. We can simplify this with a funnel-shaped cylinder for each socket. The eyes are approximately one eye's width apart.

 Instead of always drawing eyes as perfect circles, it's important to understand the movement and shape of the eyelids. From the side, an eye usually looks wedge-shaped, because that's how much of it the lids have revealed.

 Rather than using circles or ovals, the lids and lashes give us wavy lines and angular cuts, which we can use when stylizing the shape of the eye.

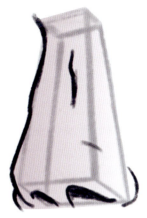

The nose is primarily a constructed rectangular prism, but in the details, we might round out the lateral or vertical shape of the nose to be more curved. On some noses, it makes sense to consider the bottom portion that includes the nostrils as another constructed box.

There's a huge variety of natural noses throughout humankind, and they can add a ton of personality or interest to your characters. Try to study and build noses into lots of different shapes.

It is always easier to have a good idea of the placement and proportion of these things first, then we can go back and add details like the nostrils and eyelids, along with eyebrows and eyelashes.

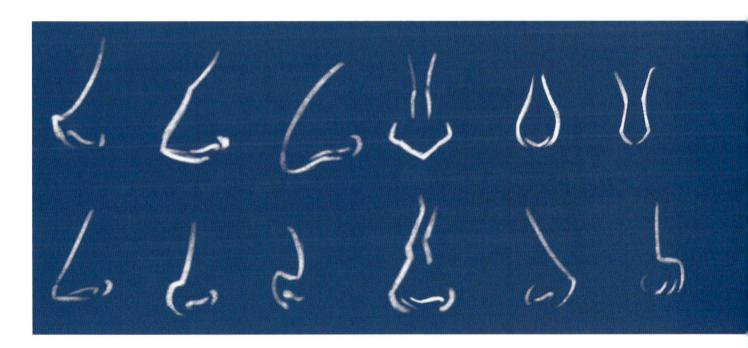

ADDING GESTURE

Since we've learned how to draw the head using construction, and have now practiced using it, does that mean it's the ONLY way we should approach drawing it? Not at all! We've done something crucial, however: we've added some backspin to your drawings. What does that mean? Biko, throw a ball in front of you with some backspin!

We can see that the ball lands in front of Biko, but because it's spinning backward, it will roll back toward him. This is what will happen now that we know how to draw the head "the right way." We can make wilder and more extreme ideas make sense. We will throw the idea out there, in the form of wackier, abstract, and extreme shapes, but we'll hone it back in with our better understanding. In our first warm-ups in Chapter One, we made tight and controlled straight lines and shapes, then followed them up with abstract and silly shapes to loosen up. We will do the same thing now, with gesture.

Okay!

Gesture is conveyed through the energy, motion, force, and weight present in a drawing. It's characteristically comprised of swooping arcs, S-shapes, and lines of action.

We will use this as we learn to draw the rest of the body, but it's also what we can use for our heads. Think about the distribution of weight in the head, and what kinds of shapes we can make, then graft the "correct" construction back on top of this.

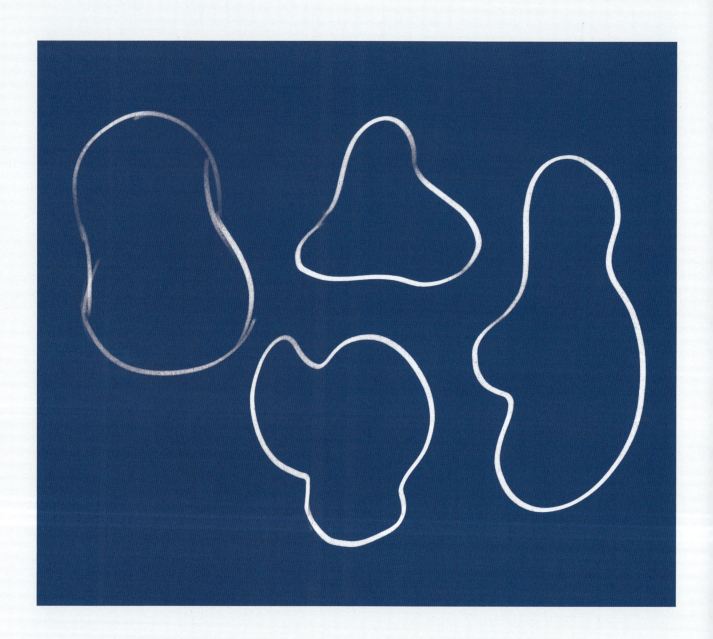

You have likely drawn the features of the face many times during your previous 50 heads practice. These features can be exaggerated, simplified, or stylized as you play with the shapes of the head. Everything you drew "the right way" has been an investment in your understanding of these things that is paying off now.

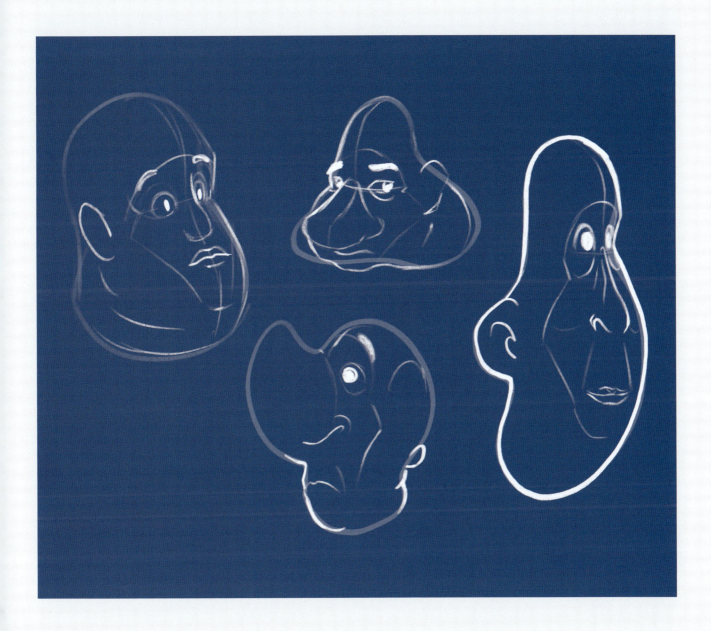

Gestural Flow

It is far easier and more possible to start with gesture in broad shapes, and refine it toward construction, than it is to start with the building blocks of constructed shapes, and then try to infuse the energy and motion of gesture. That's why we'll look at the gestural flow of the body first. These lines are incredibly easy to lay down, and can be done in a few seconds once we're used to them.

We start with an S-curve representing the spine (1), a straight line on top (2), and bottom (3) for the shoulders and hips, a cross pointing in the direction of the face for the head (6) , and four limbs (4 and 5). The hands and feet can be two little lines to cap off the limbs.

 These flowing lines can be found in the anatomy of the body, simplified as "S" or "C"-curves. The spine is a gentle S-curve.

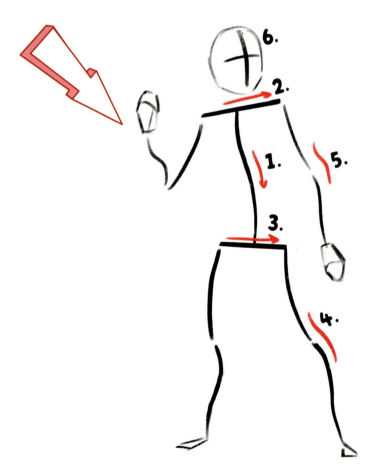

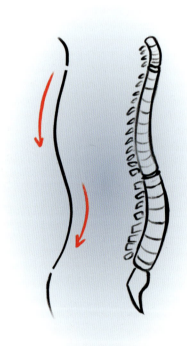

**S-CURVE
(SPINE)**

We can make sense of these anatomically later, but for now it's important to note just how much information these poses can capture, very quickly, and we haven't even added skin, muscle, or fat layers on top of the figure yet.

The arms start as C-curves out from the body for the upper half, and a small S-curve for the forearm.

 This repeats for the legs, which are again a combination of a C-curve and an S-curve.

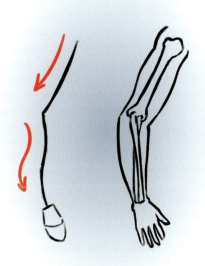

C+S-CURVE (ARMS)

C+S-CURVE (LEGS)

That's it, Biko! Find the flow!

Exercise

Spend only 60 seconds per drawing studying a pose from a photograph, or a willing nearby friend. There are plenty of websites that offer gesture drawing reference, both clothed and unclothed. Notice how the simple curves we are using ring true with the reference we're studying from. Keep the drawings quick, and do 10–20 of them.

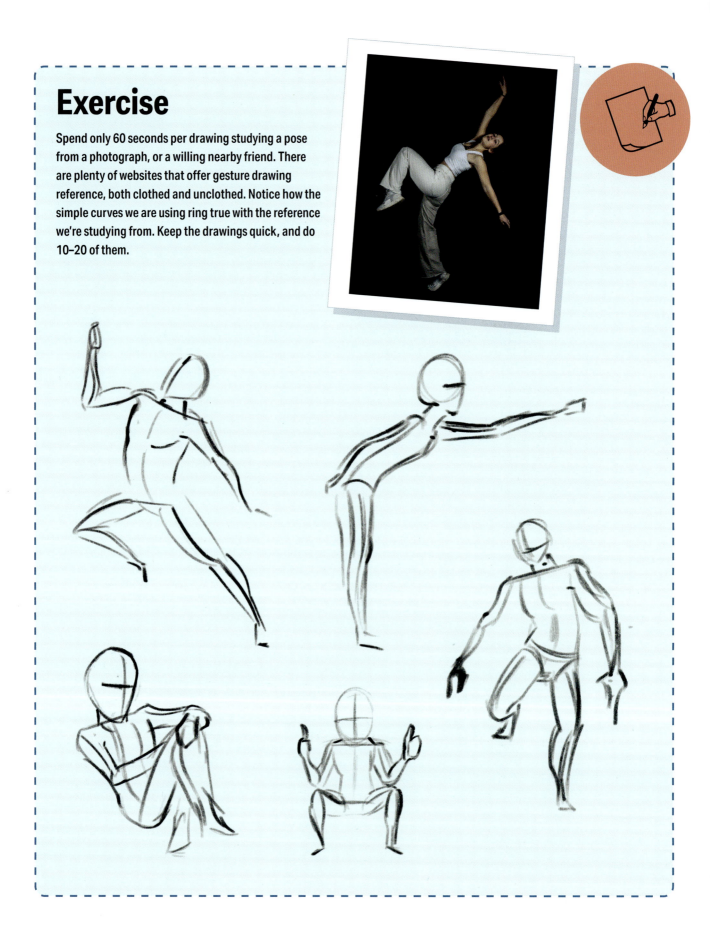

BODY CONSTRUCTION

Since we have simple gesture lines established for the body, now take a look at what kind of construction the body is made up of. The more you study the realistic forms, bones, muscles, etc., the better your drawings will be. While this section is simplified compared to all there is to know about this subject, do not do yourself the disservice of stopping your study here. Continue to practice and study to deepen and unlock your understanding.

I've been told I'm greater than the sum of my parts.

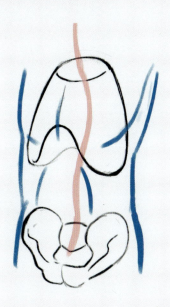

The two lines that cap off the spine in our gesture drawing on the previous page (lines 2 and 3), represent the shoulders and hips. These make up the forms of the rib cage and pelvis. These two forms can twist and bend around, and provide the body with lots of its motion and force.

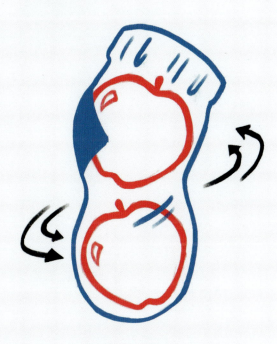

 I like to think of these two forms like two apples that have been put into a sock. They are separate pieces that are being held together to become a larger overall structure.

These are complex constructed shapes, made up of lots of pieces, but functionally, we mainly just need to remember a few characteristics. The rib cage and shoulder girdle, the upper half of the torso, can be simplified into a tapered cylinder. The ribs are lower on the sides than they are in the middle. It's important to remember that the top of this torso is slanted forward. Feel the difference in height between your clavicle (collar bones) and the base of your neck in the back, which is higher.

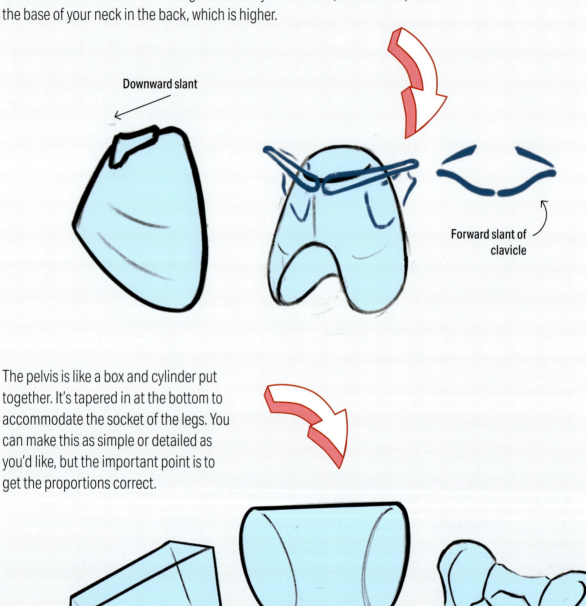

Downward slant

Forward slant of clavicle

The pelvis is like a box and cylinder put together. It's tapered in at the bottom to accommodate the socket of the legs. You can make this as simple or detailed as you'd like, but the important point is to get the proportions correct.

Tapered shape

Even though we are using constructed shapes, torsos can vary wildly in shape and size depending on if they're muscular, short or tall, relaxed or tense, or many other factors. We'll spend a lot of time exaggerating the silhouette of our character in Chapter Four, but remember you can start to use large gestural shapes to outline the torso, much like we did with the head.

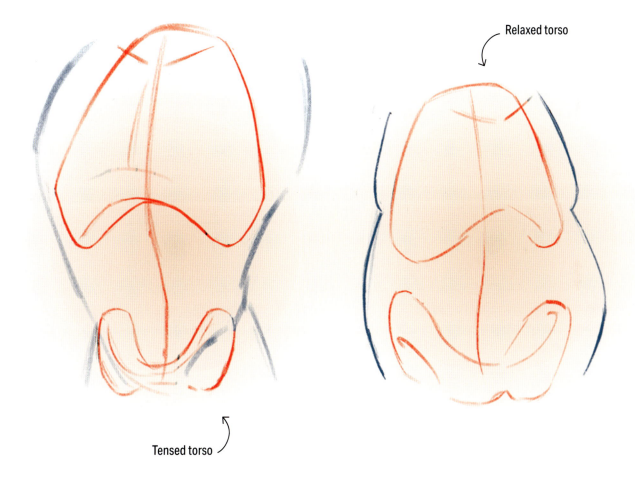

Relaxed torso

Tensed torso

Arms and Legs

Arms and legs both bend at the middle, but they also curve slightly back and forth, like our S-curves earlier. While they are both appendages, treat arms and legs differently in your studies.

For example, the shoulder has a much bigger range of movement than the hip. The elbow is simply the end of the forearm, while the kneecap is its own floating bone. The uses for arms and legs are different, so their design should be different as well.

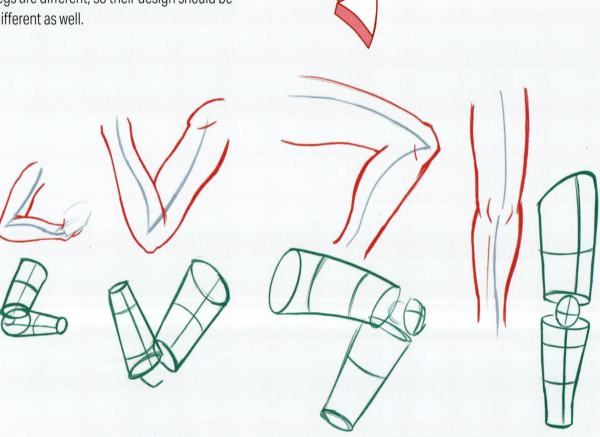

Elbow bends sharply

Kneecap joins two separate sections

The muscles on each side of the upper arm are opposites. When the arm is curled in, the bicep will contract and grow toward the bottom of the upper arm.

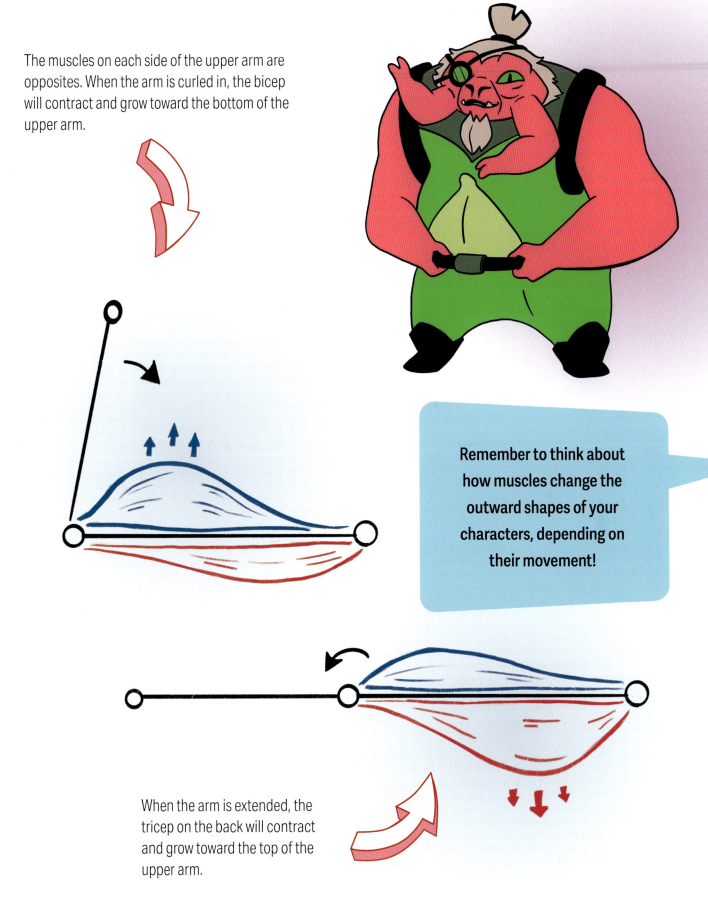

Remember to think about how muscles change the outward shapes of your characters, depending on their movement!

When the arm is extended, the tricep on the back will contract and grow toward the top of the upper arm.

Hands

Artists of all skill levels are intimidated by hands. Simplifying them helps us to understand them, and therefore draw them better. Here are three big sections of the hand:

The fingers are all different lengths, which means they make a curve at their tip.

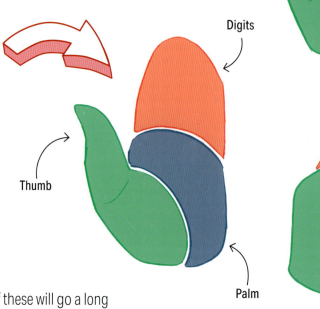

Digits

Thumb

Palm

Remembering the proportions of these will go a long way in making your hands look good. Remember that the fingers and knuckles aren't straight and uniform. The knuckles are diagonal at the base of the fingers, sloping downward out from the body.

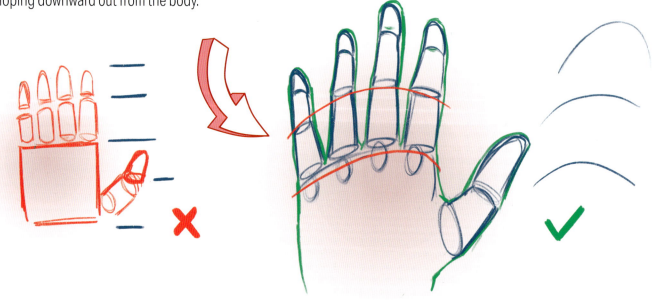

 Drawing a mitt shape that moves and flexes to different poses and expressions of the hand, lets you add in the details of the individual fingers later. Try to let them all follow a similar motion, instead of drawing them each individually. You can then allow one finger, like the pinky, to have some flair, posed slightly differently, to add some interest.

Feet

It's important for the feet we draw to "ground" our characters, rather literally. Knowing where the ground plane is, usually the flat surface our character is standing on, helps us get the right perspective, and represent our character's weight appropriately. Even if one foot is off the ground!

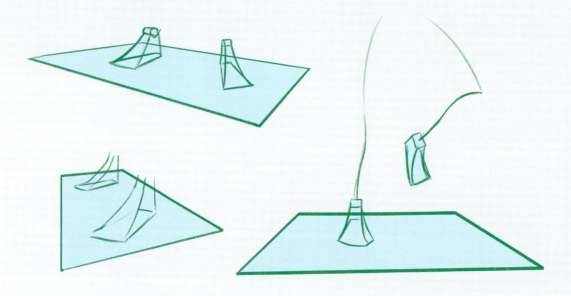

The shapes of the foot are defined mostly by the heel in the back and arch of the foot making up the majority of the structure. Then, like the fingers, our toes slope from biggest to smallest, toward the outside of the body.

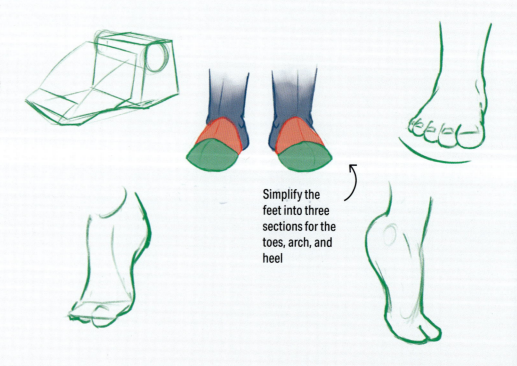

Simplify the feet into three sections for the toes, arch, and heel

The hands and feet both add a nice expressive extension to whatever limb they're attached to. An extended foot insinuates a jump, or fast motion to a leg. A hand bent back, or with fingers fanned out, compounds a lively gesture or expression.

No matter what STYLE you draw in, having a mental library of all these different parts of the body will help you draw better. As you learn and progress, revisit and study particular portions of the body to understand them deeper.

It may be helpful in the future to look at medical illustrations of things like the bones or muscles by themselves. Then, you can add your own personal stylization to them, once you've filtered them through your own brain.

If you filter something that you don't understand, or filter someone else's stylized work instead of the real deal, there's a good chance the result will come out rather wonky.

Using the method of study we applied to the human body in this chapter can be done for all subject matter! Study the real world equivalent of something in order to better draw it. Then, you can start making exaggerations, style choices, and new ideas from your imagination based on them.

SUMMARY

Combining the constructed forms of the body we've learned here, with the gesture of figure drawing, will help you to find interesting new ways to convey the human body. Again, the more you understand the body, the better your character design will be. We'll get into this more in later chapters, but look at how much you can do simply by changing the proportion of the pieces you already know how to draw.

Chapter Three:

STORY

WHAT IS A STORY?

Without story, the characters we're making are just drawings. When you see the word STORY, your mind might go to one of a few places. You might think of something that starts with "Once upon a time," or a screenplay, or lore, or a biography, or anything with a narrative structure (and you'd be right!). After all, story is present in films, shows, games, comics, and music.

But how is this illustration of a lamb in a field storytelling? It doesn't have a beginning, middle, and end!

But story can be a lot more than that, and it's important that we understand what story is, since the characters we design are vessels for storytelling. Broader than anything narrative, story is about COMMUNICATING IDEAS, and the way we go about doing that.

Drawing, illustration, comics, storyboards, animation, and just about everything you can think of that uses images to convey something, are all examples of VISUAL STORYTELLING. This is an easy thing to overthink.

That's true, Biko! However, there are clear IDEAS being COMMUNICATED in this image. The color and light, the serene pastural setting, the character's posture and expression, the prop he's holding, even the shape of the clouds, all tell us something that we can intuit visually. It may not have a beginning, middle, and end, like a story you tell verbally or sequentially, but it makes us think and feel something, no matter how simple.

This is compounded if the illustration is of a character you're familiar with, perhaps it reaffirms something about them, or challenges that instead! This is part of why fan art of characters that are already well loved tend to do so well—sometimes it's about seeing those characters in new art styles, but often it's because it's reinforcing or reminding the person seeing it of something they already know.

Visual storytelling is a broad and sometimes abstract concept, where we use things both familiar and unfamiliar to our audience to convey an idea, or many ideas. This can be as simple as an individual illustration of one character, or as complex as a decades-long animated series. In all of these cases, we use characters as vessels to show and tell the story. Let's talk about some principles that will help our storytelling, and make us better character designers.

Personification

Are all characters innately human? Some stories are indeed filled with casts of human characters, whereas others might be made up of dogs, toys, birds, aliens, or robots. Obviously then, we don't mean that all characters are literal human beings.

Let's start with something fundamental that's always true: characters are MADE by humans. Even when people claim that a machine made something, it's always "borrowing" work that humans made. And even those machines were programmed and built by humans.

If you walked outside and picked a rock up off the ground, it's just a rock. But if you started talking in a silly voice to annoy your friend, or drew two eyes and a mouth on it, that "rock" has now been imbued with human qualities. There's a word for this, and it's PERSONIFICATION. We even personify our pets and animals. We give them names, and interpret wagging tails as happiness, whimpers as sadness, and their physical affection as love. We're projecting ideas that may or may not actually be true from that pet's point of view.

Actually, I'm not a human at all, I'm a gelatinous being called a Poulticeborn!

I'm not... personified... am I?

You are, Biko! In more ways than I can probably count. Even though you're green and have floppy ears, you have a face I can identify with, you speak in a language I can understand, you react and emote the way that a person would!

Personification is about giving life to something that otherwise might not have it, but it's also the lens with which we INTERPRET and RELATE to things so that they make sense to us. When it comes to visual storytelling, we can use this to our advantage. Feature length animated films about actual toys, fish, or robots likely wouldn't be as exciting or resonant with audiences if the characters weren't heavily and intentionally personified, representative OF human thoughts, experiences, and feelings. This makes the experience of these stories more meaningful.

For us, when we share a story, we want it to matter not just to us, but to the people we share it with. Character Design goes a long way in showing something about a character.

What are stories ABOUT?

Most people would probably say that stories are "about" a set of events, or a plot, or things that happen. Maybe their favorite stories solve a mystery, have a lot of action, or have the happy couple finally get together in the end. However, those things are all external. No matter how interesting those events might be, they don't drive a good story.

A good story has a message it wants to convey, a worldview it shines a light on; an experience that's authentic to someone or some group. A story is driven by change, conflict, and a core message, set of principles, truths, or meaningful feeling that the creator wants to communicate. Without these things, a story is ultimately forgettable and lifeless. The best storytellers hone in on what their story is ABOUT, and trim out EVERYTHING else that doesn't contribute to it.

For example, here's an event that's part of a small, simple story: someone is handing a piece of food to an animal.

What's not present in this example is anything about what we should feel. What are the motives of the person giving the animal food? Is it someone rewarding a pet with a treat? Are they nursing an animal back from the brink of starvation? Are they bribing or tricking the animal into something it doesn't want to do? Each of these scenarios make us feel differently about what is happening. And as visual storytellers, we convey the stories in different ways to help sell that idea more clearly.

 Giving the pet a treat might be bright, cheery, perhaps a little mundane. The two characters can be on equal ground, perhaps in an apartment. The expressions on their faces might show glee. For conflict, maybe the pet is happy, but the owner looks exhausted or frustrated. For our audience, this scene is probably RELATABLE if they have or have had a pet. We might have made this because we want to show some "truth" about pet ownership.

 Nursing an animal back to health might make our image more dire. Perhaps it's dark and rainy, the animal barely hanging on, the human rushing to help them. There's conflict in everything that's keeping the person from being able to help the animal. The point or meaning behind the story we're telling might be to inspire pity in our audience, to make them feel for the animal, or to make them think the person is good. How we frame the image, and who the EMPHASIS is put on, will affect our storytelling.

 Bribing or tricking an animal may make our image feel insidious. Maybe the animal is in a cage, gnashing their teeth through the bars, while the human stands dangling the treat. Perhaps they have villainous traits, and we can see their conniving expression, or some hint at why they have this malicious intent. We can even use the lighting to throw a negative cast on our human character. Our audience might interpret this image as one that communicates how evil or nefarious the character is. Alternatively, our human character could have good intentions, but the animal seems unintelligent or lazy. What's important is that there is some amount of interesting CONFLICT or contrast that compels the meaning of this image.

THEME

The MESSAGE or MEANING of a story is strongest when it can be summed up in a sentence. That sentence should then be the backbone that every part of the story should reflect. A single word is not enough to be a theme—a word like "revenge" starts to convey an idea, but what exactly about revenge are you trying to say?

Is the story about how revenge is good, bad, ends up a particular way? "Revenge destroys the person enacting it more than the victim," is a theme you could build a story around. "The best revenge is a life well lived," could also work well as a story. Much like a debate or argument, showing a conflict in views or experiences between different characters is a great way to prove this point.

Storytelling

Many stories are as simple as good versus evil, selflessness and compassion versus selfishness. To see a character that did the right thing, helped others, or was resilient in the face of bad things succeed, we resonate with and might even feel some catharsis.

Honest and truthful storytelling, which might come from your own experience or perspective, will feel authentic to its audience. However, a theme that is shoehorned into a story, one that doesn't make sense, or forcefully making a propagandistic idea the meaning of the story, will weaken and cheapen it.

Everything that contributes to the story makes it stronger. Everything that takes away from the story makes it weaker. If you are a visual artist, you might feel the temptation to make something that looks cool, and rush to add a story later. Be careful that you aren't making a weak story to serve a strong drawing or design.

 One way to convey the theme of a story is through THESIS, ANTITHESIS, and SYNTHESIS.

Thesis: one character or group possess one view, perhaps extreme.

Antithesis: another, perhaps opposing character or group, possesses a different and likely OPPOSITE view of the thesis.

Synthesis: in the end, the truth comes out. The "correct" idea comes from a mix of both sides—who is right and wrong? Is it a little of both? As the person telling this story, you decide—and that's the whole point.

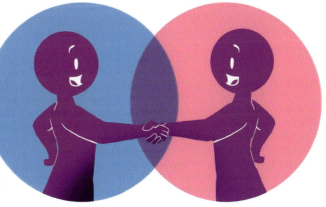

Stakes

Unless your story is a situational comedy or slice of life, where there are often simply no stakes (or stakes small enough that they can easily be returned to the status quo), there needs to be a reason why people should engage with your story. What is going to happen if the protagonist doesn't succeed or goes wrong? What are the reasons for the story to matter? Can the audience relate to them?

The most common and direct way for people to care about your story is for the stakes to be LIFE or DEATH. This doesn't necessarily mean a physical, literal death. Your characters could be battling evil forces or lethal weather, lost in space, or struggling to hold onto life during sickness. There are other kinds of death, though. Mental, emotional, and moral death are all compelling stakes in a story. A character who refuses to kill others will be faced with moral death if their opponent tempts them, or makes killing their only chance of overcoming them. Loss of a job or failure of a career is its own kind of death in a story about business.

Stakes build tension, danger, and excitement for our audience, who will stick with our characters on their journey if they feel like the situation has enough merit to be invested.

CHARACTERS

Good narrative stories show change or growth. This can happen externally (events) or internally (character arcs). If a character changes, good or bad, over the course of a story, they have a character arc, and are known as DYNAMIC characters. However, if a character is just the same at the end as they were on page one or scene one, this is a STATIC character.

Neither of these are bad, but we need to pay close attention to how we use them. If a character doesn't change, but they affect the world around them, this is still change. This can still be a good story. If the things that happen in a story are minimal or uneventful, but the character changes, this can also still be a good story. What we DON'T want is a story where nothing changes. What's the point of engaging with something if there's nothing interesting to resonate with?

Is this a static story? Nothing's happening.

I... suppose, Biko.

Archetypes

Making clear, meaningful stories, no matter what size, format, or scale they are, takes a lot of work, especially when we are using visual storytelling. Comics, animation, game development, and the like are all very time-consuming processes. Most artists will do anything that CAN save time without detracting from the quality of the story. We call this: ECONOMIC STORYTELLING. Using archetypes as a starting point for character and plot development is helpful for a number of reasons.

That's different from storytelling about the economy, Biko.

 An archetype character is one that reflects a familiar, long-established kind of character, that the audience can recognize as having certain qualities: KNIGHT. COWBOY. PRINCESS. CON-ARTIST. WISE OLD MAN.

If our character reflects some of these broad strokes, we are telling the reader what to expect from them. It's up to us whether we affirm those preconceived ideas, or subvert expectations.

What do we expect from a cowboy, for example? Wide-brimmed hat, boots, a vest or dusty clothing, maybe chaps and spurs. But we also expect a certain kind of personality; perhaps they are stoic, aloof, cavalier. If we presented a cowboy in our visual storytelling, starting with that archetype, but then changed something about them—maybe they're missing an arm, are wearing unorthodox clothes, or have the kind of personality that's very emotionally sensitive, wearing their heart on their sleeves—we've now diverged from the archetype into something that could be interesting.

One of the most famous movies ever made presents us first with a shriveled, impish old green alien, but then reveals to us that he's a wise and legendary warrior. A point is made to the main character about not judging by appearance.

Mirror Characters

We can use other characters as a great way to tell an audience about another, perhaps main, character. This could include a character that is their doppelgänger, a look-alike with an opposite personality, like your character is literally looking in an evil mirror. This would be a great way to show THESIS and ANTITHESIS.

However, mirror characters can be more than that. A second character that is similar to our first, or even EXACTLY the same barring ONE small difference, helps us to highlight that difference. Maybe this second character is older than the first, and we see the way their life has gone as a result of a certain action. They can be a warning sign, or a lesson that will help better our character.

What if royalty was just a mindset for someone living in extreme poverty?

Getting Personal

As they develop characters, different storytellers have different methods for getting to know their characters, and make them believable. Some like to flesh out every single mundane detail, down to their character's favorite cereal or favorite band in high school, others paint in broader strokes, allowing the characters to form in service of the wider story.

However you end up working, flesh out your characters with thought, as if they were real people. Base them on someone you know, possibly even someone you dislike. How could you frame a story from their perspective to make them sympathetic, or the hero?

Knowing what really motivates your characters, what their deepest fears are, why they are the way they are, not just what would be cool, will help them to feel much more real.

Looking at this character, there are a lot of context clues we get about her just from her clothing and personal items. We might ask initial questions about her like:

1. Is her day job as a mascot? And/or, did she make the dinosaur costume herself?

2. Does she go skating right after work?

3. How did she hurt her arm?

4. Is she trying to hide her identity?

5. Does she belong to a group of skaters that dress similarly, or is she a bit of an odd duck?

We can go deeper and start asking questions like:

6. What things are most important to her in life?

7. What are her ultimate wants?

8. What are her biggest obstacles?

World Building

It can be fun to figure out the rules and extra details of the world our characters live in. Some like to ruminate on the inner workings, tertiary people, and laws of physics in the fictional world they've made. Especially as visual artists, we can very easily get into the trap of fleshing out our world far too much, before we have a strong central story in mind.

Make sure to strike a balance—oftentimes those larger differences in a fictional world are big informers of your story's theme. I personally try to leave world building as a treat, where the unnecessary or far-future features of the story come after I've done the important work of figuring out the characters, their story, and so on.

When it comes to the lore, backstory, and rules of the world you're creating, the important thing is to keep in mind how it affects the characters, and what worldview or idea the world puts forward. Who benefits and who suffers because of the way this universe is? What added difficulties do our characters face because of it? What does it reflect and say about OUR world?

SUMMARY

Now that we're thinking properly about story and purpose when it comes to character, we can infuse those ideas into the visual solutions we come up with in our characters' designs. This is the fun part! Let's move into DESIGN.

Chapter Four:

DESIGN

Square shapes

COMMUNICATING THROUGH DESIGN

The previous chapters have equipped us with the tools we need in order to properly communicate whatever character designs we come up with—drawing being the HOW and story being the WHY. Logically, then, design is our WHAT.

Visual communication is present in every aspect of our lives: strings of symbols representing language form sentences and ideas, red octagons symbolize "stop," body language communicates how we're feeling, often betraying our true emotions even when our spoken words don't.

I usually like to draw the line between ART and DESIGN as the difference between EXPRESSION and COMMUNICATION, with plenty of overlap between. Art can be abstract and interpretive, the meaning left up

to the viewer. Think of how destructive it would be if a stop sign's meaning was left up to interpretation! Communicating through design is about effectively conveying an idea through principles, familiar symbols, and universal shapes.

Don't let that make character design seem boring, though! There's so much room for INTENT and STYLE as part of our work as artists and character designers. Let's take a look at some examples of design in practice and walk through the thoughts behind them.

Shape Language

Unlike a spoken or written language, shape language is NOT a set of rules. However, there's structure and meaning behind the languages we use, and freedom to wield and purposefully misuse language. We can whisper, scream, change inflection, and speak sarcastically.

In the same way, shapes are present in all character designs—there are circular, square, and angled, or triangular, shapes everywhere. As we look at these aspects of shape language, don't think of them as a set of rules, or something where we need to use only one kind of shape, or just the basic shapes themselves. Think of these as notes you can use in the music of your character design, or kinds of words you can use to infuse meaning into what you want to say.

Circular shapes

Angled shapes

Circular Shapes

The circle, as well as rounded, curved, and arcing shapes, are commonly associated with youthful, feminine, docile, and nonthreatening qualities, as well as future or latent potential. This is often the most commonly used shape language in stylized character designs, both because the organic nature of most characters lends itself to natural roundness, and because it simplifies and flows together in an appealing way for drawing and animation. Much like baby humans and animals that themselves have very round features, we are drawn to and want to take care of them.

Square Shapes

Look at how sturdy, unyielding, and structured a square is! As something of an opposite to round shapes, square shapes are often associated with strength, authority, rigidity, boredom or bureaucracy, masculinity, as well as stunted or limited emotion. Square shape language is also static, opposing round shape language's flowing and dynamic movement.

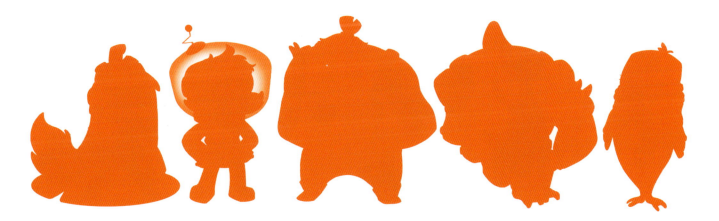

Angled or Triangular Shapes

Both angled and triangular shapes, which are interchangeable in shape language, can primarily be thought of as diagonal lines and points. There is an inherent movement and dynamism to diagonal lines. Notice the difference between an upward pointing and downward pointing triangle.

An upward pointing triangle has a lower center of gravity, it could appear hopeful, bottom heavy, or stable. A downward pointing triangle is balancing on a small point—it could appear dangerous, maniacal, or unstable. Two downward facing triangles make canine teeth—most of the danger we find in nature comes in the form of sharp carnivorous teeth, spikes, spines, claws, or quills. Even the way that characters are posed will read as triangular—when a character is in motion, or off balance, we often see their weight distributed in an angled, dynamic way.

Contrasting Shapes

As you've already seen in the body, certain shapes are echoed and balanced by others. There are S-curves that respond in order to balance out a shape. Utilizing only one kind of shape in Character Design may end up feeling repetitive and dull. We can create interest by using contrasting shapes and lines. We can also respond with a contrasting line on the other side of a shape, just like how a finger is made up of straight lines on one side, with rounded bumps for the pads of the finger on the other—one side is inherently stretched, the other is squashed. We'll talk about that more in the next section.

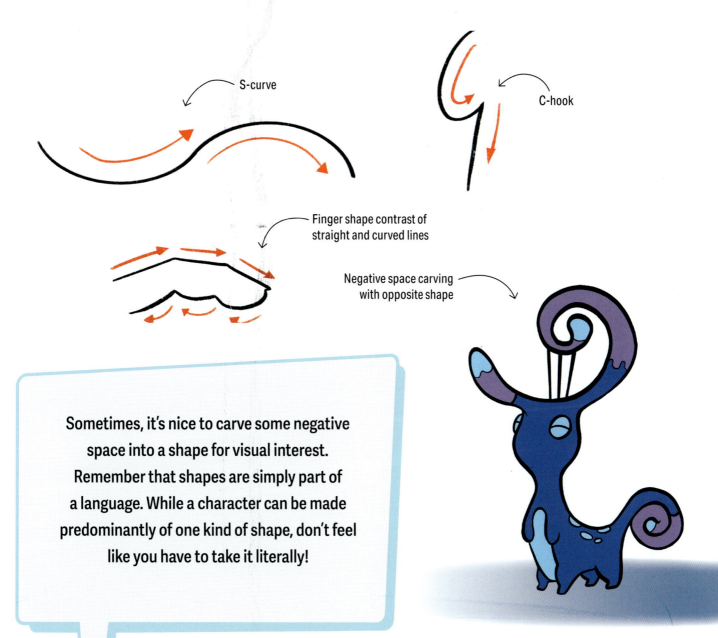

S-curve

C-hook

Finger shape contrast of straight and curved lines

Negative space carving with opposite shape

Sometimes, it's nice to carve some negative space into a shape for visual interest. Remember that shapes are simply part of a language. While a character can be made predominantly of one kind of shape, don't feel like you have to take it literally!

ABSTRACTION

It's time for our lessons in drawing to start coming into play. As character designers, there's a big secret we're holding onto, so please don't tell anyone else.

When we're tasked with making a character, let's say a rabbit character, if we aren't creating a 1:1 realistic rabbit, we aren't making a rabbit at all. Instead, we are using shapes and symbols to make a highly stylized and often simplified character that resembles a rabbit. This is called ABSTRACTION.

Abstraction has a lot to do with simplification, but more than that, it's about boiling down something to its essence in an appealing way. It also means adding features that make a character more relatable or specific, as well. Like we talked about with personification, we imbue human traits or otherwise onto our characters. When we design a creature, inanimate object, or concept to be more human, that's called ANTHROPOMORPHISM: giving something the voice, expressions, feelings, or proportions of a human.

Like, classified character designer intel?

With the character below, each version is further abstracted away from a real human. Each one has their own advantages in telling a visual story. Even though it's simpler, the example on the far right can be more expressive, elastic, and might even be easier for us to draw over and over again in different angles and poses. Our choice may also be a reflection of our story or project's TONE.

With abstraction, we can use simplification and symbols to our advantage. If we were to draw a red circle with a simple green leaf on top, this registers as a fruit. Maybe even as an apple.

 However, thanks to the recognizability of these symbols, even something that doesn't traditionally register as an apple can still be an apple, like a triangle. If we add a bite taken out of it, it's even clearer.

While this particular example may not have a lot of use in our work, it shows how far we can push and change our designs to get a desired outcome our audience still understands. We can use this same idea for humans, to make new statements and ideas about who they are.

Flat Designs

Some character designs, like a particular Japanese cat, are made of completely flat shapes. There is just a hint of 3D construction in them, and they read very simply. This makes them easily recognizable and appealing to a broad audience, and perfect for use as mascots or part of a logo. However, the amount of utility, posing, and expression you could get from a flat character is rather limited.

I feel so... merchandisable!

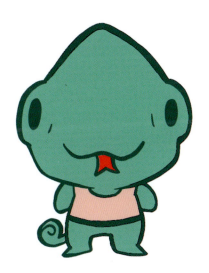

Exercise

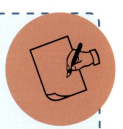

Take some time to make your own characters out of flat shapes like the ones above. Think about the limitations you have by only having them read in this flat style. Try to use line and shape as economically as possible. How much can you boil down a character before you start to lose recognizability?

Silhouettes

Speaking of overall shape, that's exactly what silhouette is—if your character was casting a perfect shadow on the wall, what would it look like?

Silhouette matters for the same reason that shape language does. What we see when we look at a character informs us about them, and the faster we can understand them, the more powerful the character is. Some of the most iconic characters in the world are instantly recognizable by silhouette. These aren't those, but they are some of my own characters.

Exercise

What overall shape does your character make in silhouette? How clear is the action that they're performing? The strength of silhouette is part of why I like to start my concepting phase for characters with small thumbnails. Using a large pencil in a small space forces me to make broad strokes that I can refine later. When we do this, there are more cohesive through-lines to the character, and less chance to muddle them with unnecessary details. Draw your own concept thumbnails using silhouettes to refine your character.

PROPORTION

Just as important as shape in character design is SIZE. The relationship in size, not only between different characters but the proportions of size within characters, is crucial for signaling what is important about a character, and for providing areas of visual rest.

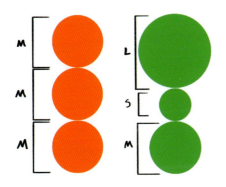

Vary PROPORTIONS with small, medium, and large areas contrasting each other, rather than lots of similar sizes. A big head might mean a character is young or smart. A large torso can represent physical strength. Large legs might imply speed or agility, and so on.

Building toward an area that's meant to be highlighted with contrasting size allows for context and anticipation.

On the left, we have several similarly medium-sized shapes in our character—it makes him all the more bland. On the right, we have a variation of large and small shapes, to break up the visual monotony. The shapes also get smaller toward the center of the character, creating some flow and importance.

APPEAL

No doubt you're familiar with something or someone referred to as being "appealing." This might mean a person is attractive, or easy to talk to, or food that looks extremely tasty. In Character Design, the quality of APPEAL includes these things, but it doesn't stop there. Appeal, more broadly, means that a design is successfully selling an idea. A character could have good appeal by being the right amount of ugly, grotesque, or scary. Appeal comes across in confident, unapologetic designs, where the designer communicated an idea thoroughly and clearly.

 Simplified shapes make an already cute animal character further sell their appeal!

 The fewer details a human character has, the more details we project onto them.

 A pet we love in real life can get pushed into further appeal with accentuated, stylized features.

I like to go a bit further with my personal definition of appeal—it actually becomes something that's physically trackable. Remember, the easier it is to look at and understand a design, the clearer and more resonant it is. That's why I think of a design as being especially appealing when multiple lines and shapes flow in the same pattern or direction. For example:

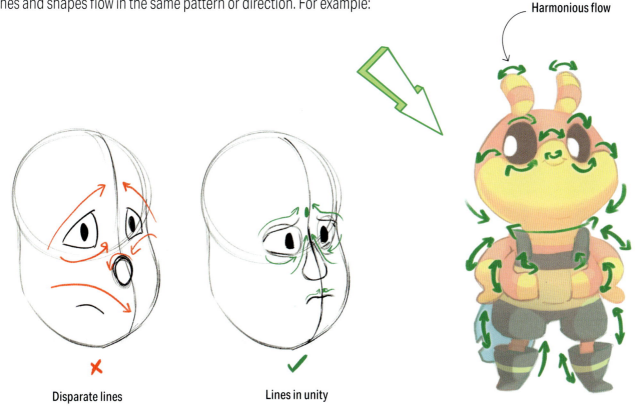

Harmonious flow

Disparate lines

Lines in unity

 When one line or shape describes multiple elements of a face or design, it feels more planned, like the shapes can flow easier, and in turn, are literally easier to look at. Our eye can follow the motions of the lines that are flowing in UNITY on the right more easily, which makes it inherently more appealing. The lines on the left are DISPARATE, and struggle to make us feel strongly one way or another.

SUMMARY

Look for ways to unify ideas in your design to make them less of a complex visual salad. In the next section, we'll look at ways to HEIGHTEN the REALITY of our designs, through exaggeration, poses, and expressions.

Chapter Five:

PUSHING DESIGN

HEIGHTEN THE REALITY

Consider this to be Part Two in our focus on design. You will sometimes hear character designers talk about ways to "push" a design. That can mean a lot of things, but most often it means some form of EXAGGERATION to make something clearer or stronger.

Character Design by nature is heightening the personality, shape, size, even color of what we know and expect in reality. Exaggeration lets us move past the limits of reality for dynamic, over-the-top, and memorable designs.

Here we can see all of the ways something in a neutral or default state (a simple square) can be pushed (or pulled!) into an exaggerated state.

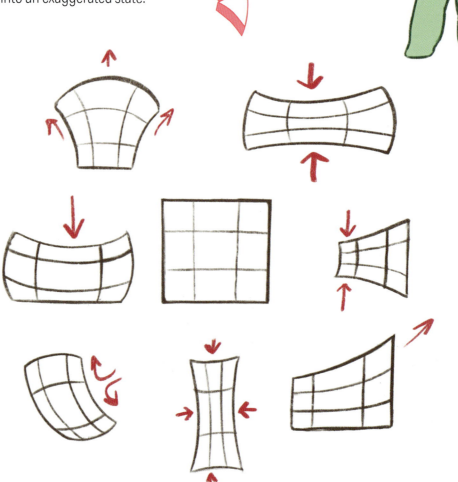

Squash and Stretch

A longtime principle of animation, squash and stretch makes our shapes and masses malleable. This can be extremely helpful to push character poses and expressions past what they could be in real life.

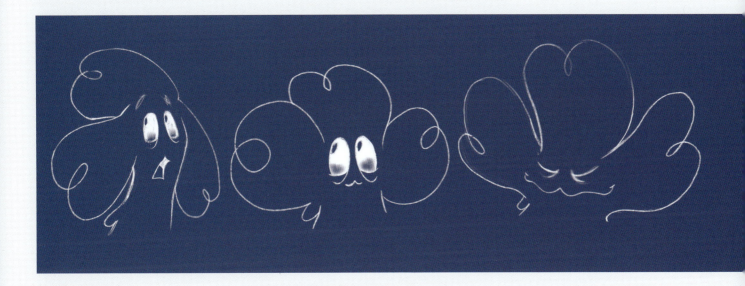

Beyond just stretching something in one direction, think about the advanced ways that we can use these principles—if we choose one point in a face, for instance, we can scrunch the rest of the face inward toward that point, or stretch it outward.

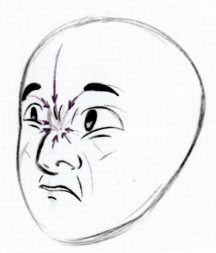

We can also utilize arcs and lines of action to plot
our squash and stretch along a curving line.

Here is where our gesture comes in handy again (see Chapter Two: Adding Gesture).
Remember that gesture is not about accurately portraying something structurally, rather
about capturing the motion and energy. We can push that energy with these squash and
stretch principles.

Dynamic Posing

An easy way to think of dynamic drawings is to substitute it with the word DIAGONAL. Oftentimes, something is dynamic when it is off-balance, off-kilter, or currently in progress. A character might be balanced on one foot mid-stride, free-falling through the air, or trying to flail their arms to rebalance themselves.

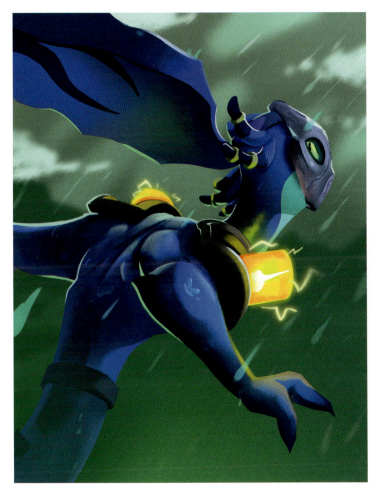

We can use a dynamic pose to convey speed, or other forms of heightened energy. Think of the forms of your character as malleable and elastic.

Depending on the level of stylization you're able to get away with, you can push the shapes, mass, and poses into extreme territories.

Acting and Expression

Remember that your characters show emotion with more than their facial expression, oftentimes their BODY LANGUAGE betrays more than their face! I like to think that most body language can be boiled down to two kinds of arcs, one forward facing and one backward facing. Each of these, matched with the right facial expression and motion, could convey a large variety of emotions.

A spine or line of action that's arcing backward could convey:

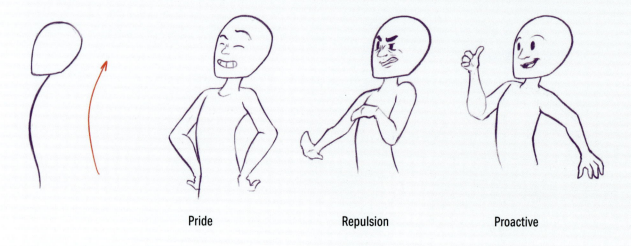

Pride   Repulsion   Proactive

While a spine or line of action that's arcing forward could convey:

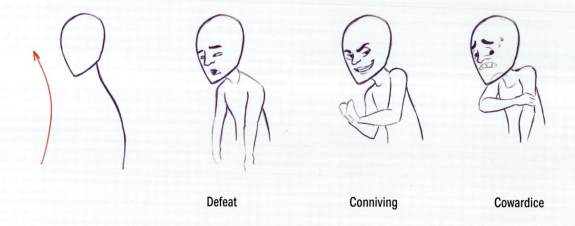

Defeat   Conniving   Cowardice

Some of these are REACTIVE and some are PROACTIVE. Either way, think of how the body can convey or betray a character's motivation or emotional state.

One of the best ways to explore expression and posing is by studying, not photographs, but video and film. That's because these sources aren't motionless poses, which tend to be static, but are always in motion, which is far more dynamic.

Exercise

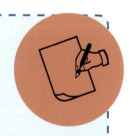

Take screenshots from a video of someone in motion. They could be playing a sport, dancing, fighting, or putting on some kind of performance. Find the gesture in these images, and look for ways to push and simplify the action to be more heightened and clear.

The Mask of the Face

Expression and emotion are most prominent in the eyes and surrounding area. It's what we look to in each other to understand how someone is feeling. The area that we learned to draw around the eye sockets, including the eyebrows and cheeks, form a malleable shape like the domino mask of a superhero. When we push and pull on this shape, along with the eyelids, we get a multitude of expressions.

Look at these sets of eyes. What emotions are being conveyed here?

The rest of the face also helps us to convey expression. Note how each facial feature can act individually, and how, in combination with other features, it can sum up an expression as a whole. The nose can scrunch upward, often in anger or disgust. This will cause the eyebrows to knit together, so most of the face starts pulling toward the center.

The mouth, of course, can show smiles, frowns, bared teeth, and pursed lips, but don't be afraid to pull the mouth toward either of its corners to help sell an expression. Don't forget to show some teeth!

Since we're already trying to use appeal in our faces, where multiple shapes of the facial features have unifying lines or patterns, we can PUSH and PULL the face as a whole around these shapes to make expressions more dynamic.

Exercise

Find a piece of acting or character you love from a film or show. Screenshot particular expressions or moods, and try to recreate their facial expressions in both a realistic, AND an extremely simple, stylized way. How far can you push their expression before the face starts to "break," or look uncanny? For example, my studies below use an extremely charismatic and boisterous TV chef and a well-loved comic TV character, and the stylized versions use their expressions as a jumping-off point for extreme, animated drawings.

Breaking Characters

As part of creating characters, we want to test expressions and poses with what we've made. It's easy to make a static, one-pose drawing of a character, but oftentimes these designs will "break" when put through their paces. For example, a character may lack the capacity to emote the way that we'd like them to, or their limbs can't contort into a nimble a pose because we put the arms, which are too short, in the wrong place...

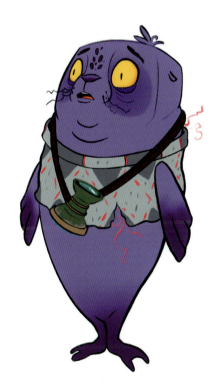

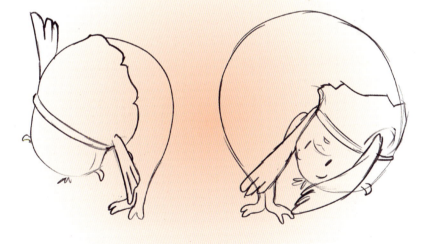

 Blubford the seal is not a particularly nimble fellow—he has tiny flipper arms and no legs to speak of.

 To get him to touch his toes, we'd need to get a bit elastic with his proportions. It's perhaps more believable in our left-hand example!

Designing our characters IN MOTION is far more valuable than starting with them drawn in a static turnaround or model sheet. That workflow utilizes our construction, to make sure their 3D shapes are dimensional and sound. However, ACTING, POSING, and EMOTION, pull on the gesture side of design to make dynamic and larger-than-life characters.

Sketches like these help to find the character's range of expression and movement, which can be especially important when they have unfamiliar shapes and proportions.

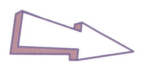

SUMMARY

Trying out our characters like this is essential, not just for stress-testing and quality assurance, but because we want to get into the minds of our characters. Will a bigger nose sell a particular emotion of our character better? Can we move their features around to have a more "punchable face," whatever that means?

Will lengthening their legs or arms make them feel more capable and qualified for the work that they do? Will tiny stub arms and legs be enough for our characters to act in an action comic we're writing? These are the questions that help a character designer to make, not just a cool drawing, but a design fit for a PURPOSE.

Chapter Six:

COLOR AND RENDERING

COLOR ROLES

Color plays an important part in the design of our characters. We might also be interested in how to make our character sketches into a finished piece. This last section of the book tackles how value, hue, light, and digital aids—like layer blending modes—can put the finishing touches on our characters.

Value

No matter what, all colors have an inherent quality called VALUE. You might think of value as how light or dark something is.

 Two values that are far apart on this sliding scale have HIGH CONTRAST. The black and the white values lie at either end of this scale, when they are are next to each other, or in the same image, they oppose each other and stand out.

 Two values that are close together on this sliding scale have LOW CONTRAST. Perhaps two grays that are quite similar. Your eye needs a bit more help discerning the difference between these two.

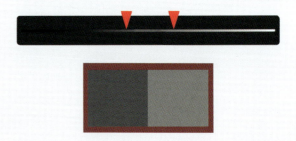

A good use of values will use high contrast to pull our eyes toward the focal points, or areas of interest, and use low contrast areas as set dressing, visual rest, and to be less important than our focal point.

Light values in the background make our main character stand out as the subject matter.

By putting two high-contrast values next to each other, for example, the mask and head around it, we call attention to that part of the image first.

The snow makes most things in this environment a very light value—we can balance that with light, shadow, and the local colors of our character.

We can use value to evoke a mood. Here, a partially shadowed fruit butcher makes unnecessarily scary work of a large melon.

In character designs, this tends to make sense as well. Oftentimes the eyes are drawn with white or very light-value sclera (the whites of our eyes) and black or very dark-value pupils and eyelashes. This concentrated contrast gives us an extra reason to look to the eyes for importance.

That's great for black-and-white drawings, but what if I want to use color?

Great question, Biko! The thing is, ALL colors have value, not just grayscale. In this picture of a digital color picker, all colors have a light, medium, or dark value, measurable from top to bottom.

What does the value of the various line colors here do to affect the way these characters appear?

SATURATION

VALUE

The colors we use all have inherent value. And if we're having trouble with colors, nine times out of ten, what we're actually having trouble with is value. This is why you may even see some painters make their work in grayscale first and add color later! While there are many ways to approach an image, knowing what your values are early on makes for strong illustrations and visual storytelling. Let's talk about those colors, though…

Hue

HUE distinguishes what color we're looking at. When you look at a rainbow, there isn't any change in value, only in hue, as each color leads into the next. We give names to these colors, like red, blue, violet, or green—but be careful about thinking about these colors as absolute.

As designers, and especially as illustrators, color is always relative to our context, as we'll see later on. Hue is actually based on the wavelengths of light, which is how we get rainbows in the first place. Hue will still be informed by VALUE, as well as saturation—how MUCH of that hue is present in a color. Saturation is classically measured from left to right in our color picker here:

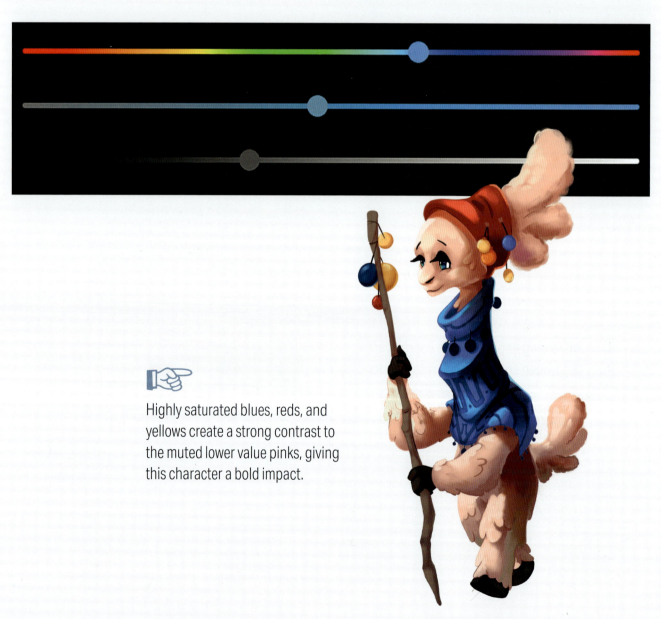

☞

Highly saturated blues, reds, and yellows create a strong contrast to the muted lower value pinks, giving this character a bold impact.

Lots of times, folks want to assemble a color palette for their character made up of their favorite colors, vibrant and all! We need to be careful how we pick out these colors, though. Remember that in value, contrast draws our eyes' attention. Which of the colors here catch your attention the most?

While certain colors like red might be a bit more dominant, you probably found it a little difficult to focus on just one color in this jumble. That's because colors with a high saturation like this tend to compete with one another visually!

Now look at what happens when we choose several muted, lower-saturation colors to go with one dominant high-saturation color.

These colors feel like they aren't competing with one another—they feel much more cohesive! Something interesting happens when our hue is very different between colors. It doesn't take much saturation for us to see a color for what it is.

In this traditional digital color picker, saturation is measured from left (none) to right (most). Be careful about picking too many colors from the top right of this box! Then you'll get a contest for attention like the first blob on the previous page.

Color is EXTREMELY relative. So, for example, this green looks pale, and almost gray, next to a high-saturation green, yet looks perfectly "green" next to a strong red!

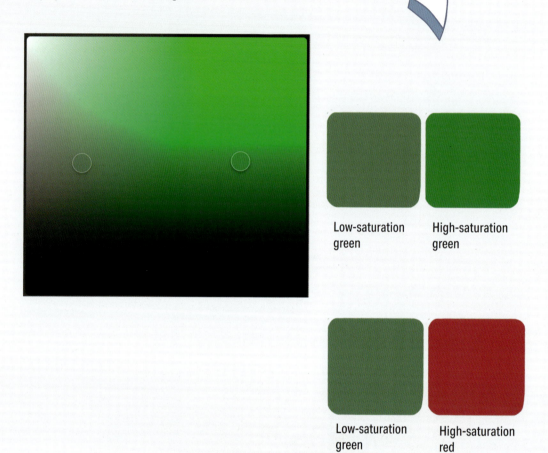

Low-saturation green

High-saturation green

Low-saturation green

High-saturation red

Use this information to construct a color palette for your character that BUILDS toward one or two strong colors. For every high-saturation color, try to complement it with neutral, low contrast, and somewhat muted colors, like grays, browns, and pastels. If you look at your surroundings, you'll likely notice that most of the world is made up of certain ranges of colors, with pops of color to get your attention. Even in nature, the greens and browns we see are all harmonious with each other.

Exercise

Take photographs, preferably outdoors. Next, load your pictures into an app or program where you can eyedrop or pick colors. Find the five most dominant colors in a handful of photos. Look to see what value and hue these colors are in your color picker. What happens when you draw on top of these pictures with a high-saturation, high-value color?

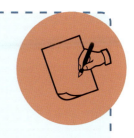

This image from a sunny day has relatively high-saturation blues and greens, but is balanced out by neutral browns.

Notice how the bubble refracts the light during this sunset shot to create more saturated pinks, blues, and greens.

The values and hues here are all very similar, and blend together easily. Be careful of brown wildlife crossing in front of the brown road if you're driving here, they'll be easy to miss!

Choosing Colors

You might be familiar with various forms of color wheels. In most cases, red, yellow, and blue are considered primary colors. Their opposites are green, purple, and orange respectively. Complementary colors are colors that oppose each other on the color wheel, and often go together well: red and green, orange and blue, yellow and violet.

When picking colors, for example, two blues, it's often good to not only change the value, such as a lighter or darker blue, but to also make a shift in hue, toward purple or green ever so slightly. This will help the colors to look less like they are bland or washed out (we'll talk about why this is in the following section on light).

However, something important to remember with color palettes is that these are only the LOCAL colors. That is, what these colors look like without taking into account anything in their environment. Perhaps if we photographed this palette in a white blank void, these would be their colors. However in reality, most colors are affected by the color and intensity of LIGHT and SHADOW.

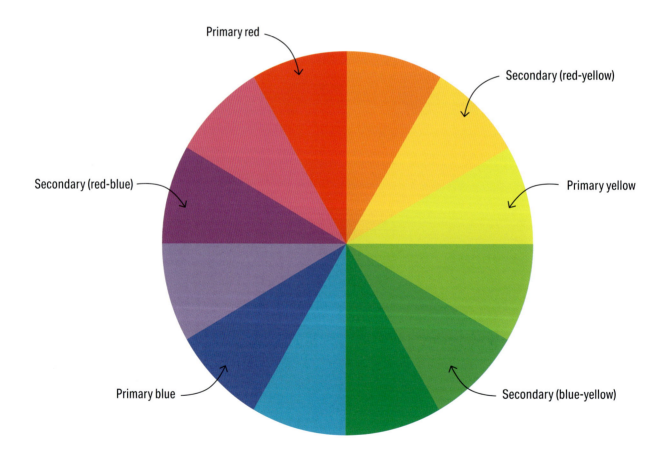

**COLOR WHEEL THAT ALIGNS PRIMARY
AND SECONDARY COLORS**

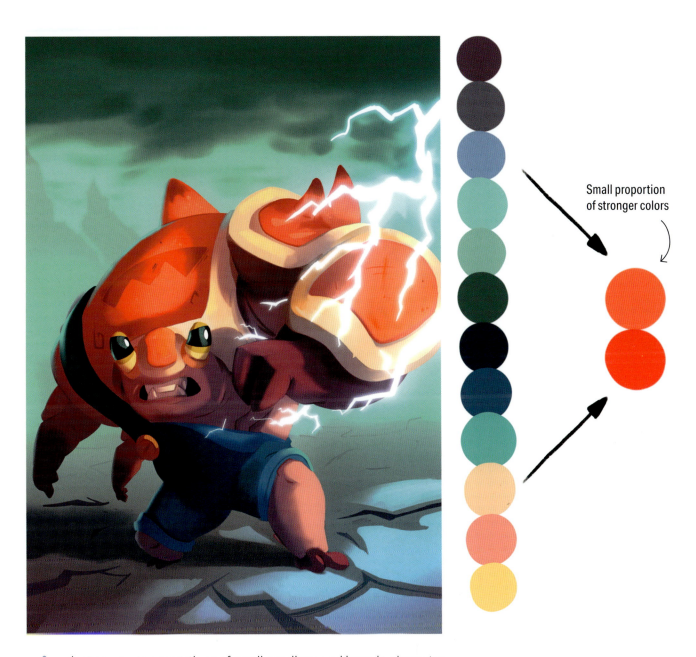

Small proportion
of stronger colors

 Just as we use proportions of small, medium, and large in character
design, it's helpful to do the same when assigning colors. Let more
of the subtle colors build toward strong colors.

LIGHT

Light bouncing off surfaces is what enables us to see things. Speaking of blank white voids, most light is NOT pure white. Our sun, for example, is typically casting yellow light, which sometimes warms toward orange or even purple, depending on how the atmosphere is affecting it.

Light hits surfaces and helps inform us of what the material of that surface is like. For cloth and matte materials, the light is softly scattered. For a rough texture like asphalt, the light leaves room for small shadows called AMBIENT OCCLUSION, in between the cracks. For a shiny or even reflective surface, the light concentrates at the point it's hitting most directly to create a SPECULAR HIGHLIGHT. For something semi-translucent like skin or even thick glass, the light penetrates the material and bounces around.

Different surfaces change the way light bounces in this image, creating several kinds of textures.

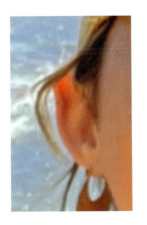

Light source
(the sun!)

Where light permeates through skin or fur (see the lamb overleaf), it diffuses to create a range of tones that merge from light to dark.

Backlit

Subsurface
scattering

The direction our light is coming from is called a LIGHT SOURCE. Many illustrations have multiple light sources, often one MAIN one, like the sun, a secondary or BOUNCE LIGHT, such as the light bouncing off the floor and back onto the subject, and often a RIM LIGHT, which highlights the edge of a subject and creates strong contrast, often giving a heightened focal point.

When your light is coming from a certain direction, it's important that the light source is consistent on all parts of your character. This is where remembering 3D construction will come in handy, since you can think about how the pieces of your character are overlapping.

There is ambient light hitting the fingers from above, but there's stronger intensity of light coming from the backlight.

 The sun from behind this lamb's ear lets us exaggerate the pink subsurface scattering toward an almost fuchsia color.

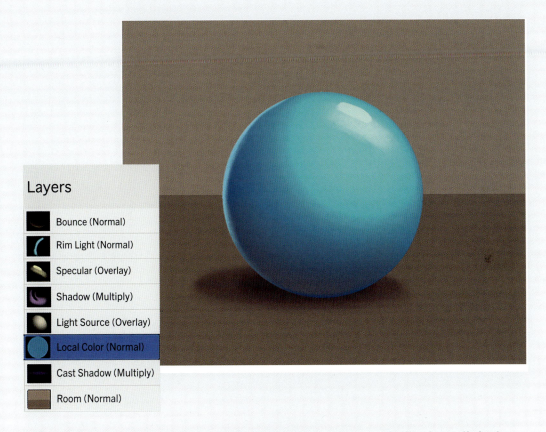

Layers

	Bounce (Normal)
	Rim Light (Normal)
	Specular (Overlay)
	Shadow (Multiply)
	Light Source (Overlay)
	Local Color (Normal)
	Cast Shadow (Multiply)
	Room (Normal)

 Here's a breakdown of what the layers might look like in a digital program like Procreate, including their blending modes. This isn't a definitive list or process, but it can be helpful to lay some of these lighting considerations first, then fine tune for your final image. It helps to consider: Nearby surfaces, angle and distance of the light, and the texture of what you're painting.

FAKE IT TILL YOU BREAK IT

It's important to be able to create realistic or believable lighting conditions in your drawings and illustrations. However, remember that you can also suspend your disbelief. If tweaking the reality of the light in your image makes for a stronger read, by all means do so! You're involved in the act of stagecraft here—as long as the audience believes it, we don't need to be strict light and shadow accountants.

Shadow

Shadow comes about as an absence of light. This is most often seen in AMBIENT OCCLUSION, mentioned earlier, and CAST SHADOWS—the kind of shadow that happens when an object is in the way of a light source. You usually make a cast shadow on the ground when there's light above you. Shadow is often an opposite, or complementary, color to the light source. This is mostly because the wavelengths of the light contrast with the shadow. However, it can also be done stylistically because it looks appealing.

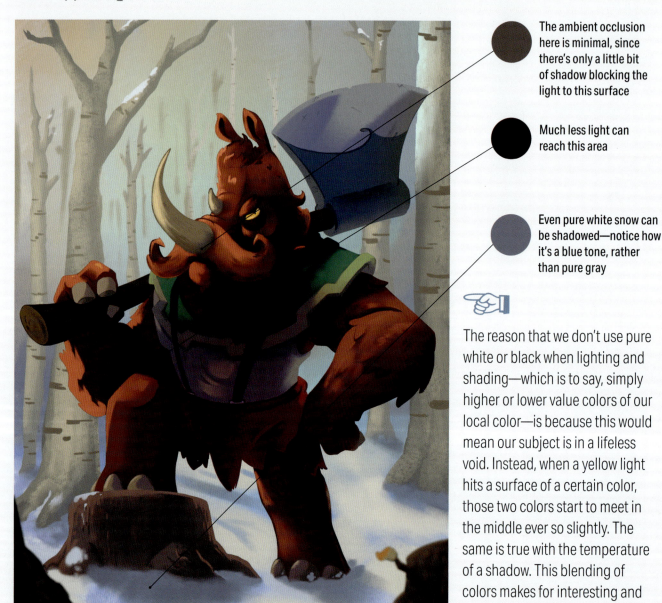

The ambient occlusion here is minimal, since there's only a little bit of shadow blocking the light to this surface

Much less light can reach this area

Even pure white snow can be shadowed—notice how it's a blue tone, rather than pure gray

The reason that we don't use pure white or black when lighting and shading—which is to say, simply higher or lower value colors of our local color—is because this would mean our subject is in a lifeless void. Instead, when a yellow light hits a surface of a certain color, those two colors start to meet in the middle ever so slightly. The same is true with the temperature of a shadow. This blending of colors makes for interesting and appealing rendering.

DECIPHERING BLENDING MODES

When it comes to digital illustration, depending on the program we use, there are a few conventionally used types of layers that can assist our illustration and rendering. Layers all stack together on top of each other, like panes of glass.

Normal:
This layer simply shows up the way we mean it to—opaque colors exactly as they were picked. Digital images are raster-based, which means we are laying down colored pixels when we draw.

Opacity:
All layers have a percentage of OPACITY, showing how transparent or translucent they are. Oftentimes, we get a better result by significantly reducing the opacity of one of the following blending modes, so that it isn't overpowering our NORMAL layers underneath it.

Overlay:
This BLENDING mode tends to affect the contrast of our image—it relies on the values in the image to push toward extremes, and uses color to build toward average hues.

Multiply:
This is a very commonly used blending mode to create SHADOW—even using a light pink or blue in a multiply layer will heavily darken what's underneath it.

Color dodge/add:
The name for this blending mode is different across programs, but think of it like shining a bright and powerful spotlight onto the pixels it's affecting, often blowing out or blooming the light around it. This mode is best utilized in sparing amounts.

Be careful not to rely too much on these layer modes! Once they help you get about halfway toward the intended look of an image, I like to start overpainting with a normal layer, on top of the rest, for simplicity.

ILLUSTRATION WALKTHROUGH 1

I'd like to show you how I approach illustration and rendering character designs. This will build from simple to complex, and you can take any part of it to use in your process. Please note that this is done digitally, with principles that work in apps like Procreate, Photoshop, Clip Studio, and so on, since most art apps utilize layers and blending modes. Personally, I use Procreate, and recommend it highly.

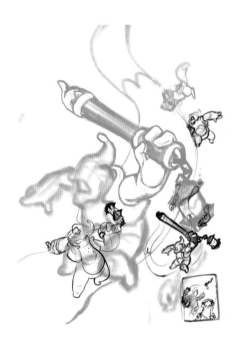

1. Sketch

Once I have a clear idea, I like to refine the sketch to a place where it's clean. I could start to draw ink lines over the top of this, or I could use it as the base of a painting. Ink will simply look more defined and comic-like. At this point, I'm usually drawing on a document that's at least 5 x 7in (13 x 18cm) and 300 dpi.

2. Ink lines

On a new layer, I'll choose an ink brush and make smooth, final lines over the top of my sketch. I like to lower the opacity of my sketch layer to see the ink lines better. NOTE: sometimes I will create ink lines even when my intention is to create a painting, as we will in this case. It helps to create defined sections of color.

3. Color flatting

Here I'll choose colors to start with, either from a predefined palette, or by choosing on the spot. Don't get too attached to these local colors, since they'll be affected by the environment and light as well, if we choose to render to that level.

4. Layers

To create lineless art from the above work, use a clipping mask over the top of the line art, make a new layer, and set it to 90 percent opacity. Now, I can pick the flat color nearest the line, but see where it meets up with the edge of another shape. Remember to think about what shape is in front of another. Lines are an abstract way of separating ideas, but now we're making shapes of color that don't have division between them.

5. Adjustments

We can duplicate our line color layer now, and bringing down the brightness a little, as well as increasing the saturation, we can keep lines where we want to, and erase the rest.

6. Shadows

Multiply layer is a quick way to lay in shadow. First, we'll duplicate our line layer and color layer. Then, we'll merge them together and lower the brightness so that it's completely black. Bring this layer to the top of the layer stack, select everything in it, then hide it. This will work as our mask over the top of our lines and shapes.

On a new layer over everything else, fill in this selection with a pastel pink or purple color. Now, set the blending mode of this layer to multiply. Immediately, we have shadow affecting everything.

This is too much, so take an eraser and cut the light shapes back out of the multiply layer. We can also lower the opacity so it isn't as intense. We can make hard shadows for a comic look, or softer ones to proceed further with painting. It's often nice to lock the opacity of our shadow later, and use a large, soft airbrush to paint a different color into a portion of our layer. For example here, we are transitioning from our purple into a blue. This shows the light temperature is changing across our figure.

7. Overpainting

From here, we can start a new normal layer and paint to our heart's content. Learning what to paint where is a whole other field of study, but I like to use this form of overpainting to fine tune the look of my drawing, and to give it more life, instead of just looking like a comic image. Don't make something too shiny unless the surface really is that way! Try to balance the light source washing over the character overall with it hitting portions of your character individually. Make sure the cast shadows and ambient occlusion are there as well.

Study different ways and styles other artists bring their characters to life! There's no one way to do this, and much of it depends on your own artistic voice and goals.

ILLUSTRATION WALKTHROUGH 2

Here is another illustration example that shows how it's not always one, linear path we need to follow:

1. Sketch

In this illustration, I started with a few sketches of a boating butterfly-inspired character named Tulston. I knew I wanted him to have an asymmetric head, and to contrast the delicate nature of butterflies with the salty, rugged spirit of an adventurer.

2. Refining

In this sketch, I get an idea of what I'd like for the illustration layout to look like. I even get to the next step and layout color and some basic lighting.

3. Revisions

However, at this point, I'm not happy with the way the image is flowing. Instead of spending more time on this version of the illustration, I go over the top of it with a new layer, and redraw the character to be more dynamic.

4. Background

Next, I use a Hard Round Brush to quickly lay in the background. It would be cool to see him boating at night, with something like the aurora borealis colored like this behind him! Nevertheless, our illustration is set simply in a sunny environment.

5. Ink lines

Next, I add ink lines to the places where I feel it will be important to get clean edges to our shapes. In the water and background, it won't be as important, especially since we'll be painting those with larger shapes instead of lines.

6. Color flatting

Next we flat our colors just the same, either from a predefined palette, or by choosing on the spot.

7. Lighting

With our sunlight coming from the upper right of the illustration, we start to see the dimension of our image.

8. Shadows

With light come shadows!

9. Final touches

The water completes our final render.

FINAL THOUGHTS

I hope the information in this book has been helpful for you. Here are some main points that are always worthwhile revisiting in your practice:

- Regularly study and brush up on your knowledge of anatomy. It will help your skills and deepen your understanding.

- Study the original thing your character or concept is based on to make you better at drawing the invented or stylized version of it.

- Think with a story in mind, and how your choices can better communicate the narrative or goal of your design.

- Look for ways to simplify, streamline, or improve your designs by increasing their appeal. Unify the ideas, shapes, and lines, or push a design further into a concept.

- Act your characters out! Make them elastic, put them through their pose-paces, and adapt the expressions you find in actors and real life.

- Think about how your choice of color and even lighting can change the mood, aesthetic, or tone of your character.

Keep these principles in mind, and you'll keep growing! Thanks for reading, and have fun creating!

ABOUT THE AUTHOR

Brookes Eggleston is a New York-based character designer and art generalist who has made a big deal about characters for quite some time now. Brookes has been regularly posting videos on the Character Design Forge channel since 2016, teaching visual storytelling, assisting students, and championing the artistic mindset while sharing his own journey of improvement along the way. He is the creator of the Learn Character Design Course and the Stormfellers Animated Series, and has worked with brands like Disney, Pinkfong, Epson, and FableVision.

ACKNOWLEDGMENTS

I'd like to thank:

My wife Tay, my parents, and my family and friends for their incredible support over the years.

Nick and John for their patient mentorship, despite a very slow student.

The folks at David and Charles for all their help and input creating this book.

Everyone who's generously given their time, attention, and trust over the years (including you, reading this book) as we all make progress on our creative journeys.

INDEX

A DAVID AND CHARLES BOOK
© David and Charles, Ltd 2025

David and Charles is an imprint of David and Charles, Ltd
Suite A, Tourism House, Pynes Hill, Exeter, EX2 5WS

Text and Art © Brookes Eggleston 2025
Layout © David and Charles, Ltd 2025

First published in the UK and USA in 2025

ISBN-13: 9781446314869 paperback
ISBN-13: 9781446314883 EPUB

This book has been printed on paper from approved
suppliers and made from pulp from sustainable sources.

Printed in China through Asia Pacific Offset for:
David and Charles, Ltd
Suite A, Tourism House, Pynes Hill, Exeter, EX2 5WS

10 9 8 7 6 5 4 3 2 1

Publishing Director: Ame Verso
Senior Commissioning Editor: Nigel Browning
Managing Editor: Jeni Chown
Editor: Victoria Allen
Copy Editors: Clare Ashton and Katie Hardwicke
Lead Designer: Sam Staddon
Designers: Lucy Ridley and Karen Constanti
Pre-press Designer: Susan Reansbury
Production Manager: Beverley Richardson

David and Charles publishes high-quality books on a
wide range of subjects. For more information visit
www.davidandcharles.com.

Share your art with us on social media using
#dandcbooks and follow us on Facebook and Instagram
by searching for @dandcbooks.

Layout of the digital edition of this book may vary
depending on reader hardware and display settings.